WITHDRAWN

Preparing for the
Back Nine of Life

ERIC PETERSON

Preparing for the
Back Nine of Life

A Boomer's Guide to Getting Retirement Ready

Published by Advantage, Charleston, South Carolina.
Member of Advantage Media Group.

ADVANTAGE is a registered trademark and the Advantage colophon is a trademark of Advantage Media Group, Inc.

Printed in the United States of America.

ISBN: 978-1-59932-477-7
LCCN: 2015932195

Book design by Megan Elger.

This publication is designed to provide accurate and authoritative information in regard to the subject matter covered. It is sold with the understanding that the publisher is not engaged in rendering legal, accounting, or other professional services. If legal advice or other expert assistance is required, the services of a competent professional person should be sought.

Advantage Media Group is proud to be a part of the Tree Neutral® program. Tree Neutral offsets the number of trees consumed in the production and printing of this book by taking proactive steps such as planting trees in direct proportion to the number of trees used to print books. To learn more about Tree Neutral, please visit **www.treeneutral.com**. To learn more about Advantage's commitment to being a responsible steward of the environment, please visit **www.advantagefamily.com/green**

Tree Neutral

Advantage Media Group is a publisher of business, self-improvement, and professional development books and online learning. We help entrepreneurs, business leaders, and professionals share their Stories, Passion, and Knowledge to help others Learn & Grow. Do you have a manuscript or book idea that you would like us to consider for publishing? Please visit **advantagefamily.com** or call **1.866.775.1696.**

*Dedicated to my Mother, Allison—the hardest working person
I've ever known. She raised three children by herself and gave me my
greatest attributes—my sense of caring, humour and empathy.*

*This is also dedicated to my Wife, Teresa, for supporting me
in building my firm and raising our two amazing children.
You are not only the love of my life, but my best friend.*

TABLE OF CONTENTS

ABOUT THE AUTHOR

Eric Peterson is the founder of Peterson Financial Group, a full-service financial advisory firm dedicated to providing cutting-edge retirement strategies and practical core values. The independent firm tailors financial plans to the individual's unique needs and goals.

A Registered Financial Consultant (RFC), Peterson is an active member of the Ed Slott Elite IRA Advisors Group, which updates participants continuously on IRA planning, distribution strategies, and current tax laws, a highly specialized area.

With a unique focus on capital preservation, Peterson Financial Group uses the best-suited tools in the industry, combining income planning, institutional wealth management, and estate planning strategies, and offers the highest-quality advice and solutions to enhance the quality of its clients' lives.

A Business of Dreams

Much of the ladies' conversation was puzzling to the little boy falling asleep in the salon chair. But it was intriguing, too, and comforting, as the chatter drifted into murmurs and then to silence.

It was 1975. My mother, a hairdresser and single mom, would take me to work with her in San Diego on days when I was too sick to go to school. Missing a day's work wasn't an option for her. She would get me settled into one of the dryer chairs, feel my forehead, and turn her attention to her clients.

It seemed to me that she only did hair for old ladies, though they doubtless thought of themselves as being in their prime. Many of them would come to her salon twice a week. Most of them, I'm sure, lived well on their husbands' pensions and Social Security benefit and gave not a thought to the rise and fall of markets and the ways of Wall Street. They were comfortable, and their lives were structured.

I would lie there, listening to the sounds of the salon: the click-clicking of scissors, the humming of blow-dryers, and the ebb and flow of the voices. They would talk about their vacations and their shopping trips and their grandchildren and their ailments. And they would talk about grown-up matters that I scarcely understood as my eyes glazed over and closed.

After a while, when I awoke and felt better, I would help out around the place, sweeping up hair and getting coffee for the ladies. I enjoyed serving them. And I liked hearing their stories. They would tell me what they were doing with their own families and friends and what they dreamed of doing. They were the retired generation, and I thought of them as my friends.

Sometimes, I would pass the hours playing with jigsaw puzzles, getting all the pieces in place to build the big picture. I liked solving things and getting it right, and I still do. I don't like leaving things to chance.

As I think of those days, it makes sense to me that my career evolved into financial planning for retirees. I still get to listen to their stories as I serve them. I'm still sweeping up the mess sometimes. And I get to work on puzzles: move that piece here, fit that one in there, and a problem is solved. Some of the pieces fall easily into place. There's no doubt about where they go and how they will function. It takes finesse to get other pieces to work well with the rest.

A happy client is a joy for me, and though I enjoy helping retirees, I don't see becoming a retiree myself. I may slow down, but I'll always want to be involved in my clients' lives. It's rewarding to help people, and in doing what I enjoy, I've been able to build a successful practice.

When I was in college in San Diego, I worked for a time as a waiter in a fine-dining restaurant. Our patrons demanded and deserved good service. They came to have a good time and to celebrate, and they were spending a lot of money to do so. Treating them well was my pleasure, and I felt gratified that some of the regulars would request that I be their waiter.

I would listen to their stories too, as I moved among the tables. They shared the details of their lives with me, just as my clients often do today. I enjoy talking and getting to know people, and I got that from my mom. No one is a stranger to her. She can talk to anyone, a good skill for a hairdresser. That's how she built a loyal clientele. She developed true bonds with her clients, and that's what kept them coming back. You can't treat people like numbers. Each has a story, with victories and setbacks, with joys and challenges. They work hard, and they save, and in everyone's life, there should be a time to celebrate.

As a retirement planner, I see people through it all. That's what it's all about. I have plenty of important paperwork to do, but I'd much rather be chatting with a client, finding out how life has been going. Money does fascinate me—how it works, how it grows, how people earn it and protect it—but we talk about a lot more than finances. We talk about fulfilling dreams. In retirement planning, I have found the perfect career.

■

The biggest fear facing retirees today is how they can make sure they have enough money to last the rest of their life. They are concerned about outliving their money. And now that they have stopped working, they wonder what to do with what they have accumulated. They are unsure of the landmines that could threaten their life's savings.

One major worry is the prospect of health-care catastrophes. They worry about having some kind of medical issue that eats up their nest egg. They may be fully aware of landmines like that, the sort of thing that Donald Rumsfeld called the known unknowns.

But other threats may lie in wait unbeknownst to them. They may not even have considered, or fully considered, what could happen. Those are the unknown unknowns, as Rumsfeld might say. They include investment risk, fees and expenses, taxes, inflation, and, of course, their own longevity and the prospect of outliving their assets, among other things.

Clients have said to me, "I don't want to be a bag lady," and "I don't want to be a burden to my children." Such fears run deep, and those who are in the boomer generation and getting ready to retire now tend to be sandwiched in between. They worry not only about their children but also about caring for their aging parents.

Parents of the older generation have had a system that worked well for them: the traditional "three-legged stool" of retirement funds that included pensions, Social Security benefit, and their own savings. And they also expected to spend less.

Their children, however, are approaching their own retirement with different expectations. For some, it amounts to "I want everything" and "I want it now." It's as if they're looking for a fountain of youth. Unlike their parents, many grew up without much of a struggle. They have no memory of the Great Depression, certainly, or of the rationing and sacrifices during World War II, and yet the echoes of hard times and war times still reverberate.

Some of those children have listened well to their parents' stories and planned accordingly. Others have not. It's not that they set out to ignore common sense. People nearing retirement age today have grown up in a culture where doing as your parents did wasn't the way to go. The independent spirit can serve a body well so long as one heeds the lessons of the past.

Some of today's retiring boomers have indeed navigated their own course with great success. They adopted what their parents did right, and they saw where their parents fell short. "Mom and Dad never got to follow their dreams," they say as they trek through Europe and take that cruise and check off the items on their bucket lists. This new crop of retirees will have a more active and fulfilling retirement—that is, if they know what they can afford and plan early to help ensure that's the case. Such freedom requires an adequate and reliable income.

A NEW PHASE OF LIFE

Retirement is a new phase of life. It's far different from one's working years when the emphasis was on accumulating for the future, on filling up the storehouse. When the retirement years are here or nigh, all that has changed. The new emphasis is on how to tap into that storehouse, perhaps for decades longer, without running it dry.

Accumulation is easy, in a sense. You have that regular paycheck coming in, and you save some of it.

It's a portion you don't need to rely upon for income. If the market goes down, so what? You don't like the way it looks on your investment statement, sure, but then again, you don't need to withdraw the money to meet your needs. What goes down comes back up in time, and more, usually. And if you don't need the money, at least for several years, your loss will be on paper only.

A critical shift occurs at retirement. No longer do you have that steady stream of paycheck income. You have to create your own paycheck. You want to know that it is guaranteed, but you cannot get a guaranteed income from a source that is not guaranteed. You can get stung badly if all your investments are in a fluctuating market.

Any financial professional will tell you that, historically, the markets have bounced back. They will give you the figures and the statistics to establish their case. And they are correct, over a long period of time. But the problem is that to know your true return, you need to subtract what you pay in investment fees and expenses and consider the toll of taxation.

You can't predict what people will do in a panic. Who knew how they would react in 2008? You can consider yourself an aggressive investor, but were you aggressive then? Over time, yes, the market will perform its historical norms. But when you add people into the mix, you are dealing with emotions, and those, as we all know, can be unpredictable. Unless you are prepared through proper planning to act wisely, the consequences to a portfolio can be devastating.

At retirement, it is time to shift the gears. It is time to move from an accumulation mindset to a strategy of protection. If you do not, you increase your risk of running short of money before you leave this earth. Sure, you might make it. But you are in choppy waters when you pull money from fluctuating investments to fund your retirement. If, like many retirees, your greatest fear is running out of money before you die, why would you want to take any chances?

HOLDING ON TO THE BRASS RING

Our clients, typically, are age 50 or greater and thinking seriously about retirement. They've been successful in accumulating their assets. They're not in accumulation mode any longer. They're conservative. They're not risk takers, at least not on all of their money. They want to enjoy retirement. They look forward to it, but they are cautiously optimistic. They want stability and predictability, and they want to dispel any anxieties they feel about retirement.

When prospects come to our office, announcing, "I need you to make me 10 percent a year," we are not the people for them. Or they may ask, "So how do you do against the Dow and the S&P?" Those are the accumulation people, and there are a lot of them out there. They are still in that orientation, looking for the win.

By the time people seek the kind of planning we do for them, they have already won. They got the brass ring on the carousel, and they're figuring out how to keep ahold of it. They won, but it's not time to step down from the ride. They intend to enjoy it for a while. By contrast, the accumulation types are still reaching out and grasping.

In this wide world of investing, some have won, some are still trying to win, and some just want the ride. Some have fumbled their ring and are trying to get it back. The game is different for each person. That's one of the biggest problems: All investors compare themselves to somebody else.

As for those who seem to want to claim the brass ring twice, they would do well to identify what they actually need in retirement. If they are willing to do so, we can help them. We have a four-step evaluation process, in which such people well might discover that they don't need to make 10 percent a year. Maybe they only need to make 4 percent to accomplish their goals. That means they can accept less risk, which is a good way to sleep better.

Often, they never have experienced that style of planning. They have been dealing with Wall Street-oriented advisors who tell them, "Throw down your money here, keep on investing, and keep your head down." Instead, people anticipating retirement need to ask, "How do I position my investments, and how much money do I actually need?" Budgeting is wisdom. Where will the money flow out, and in what streams will it flow?

Once you know the answers to those questions, you can see just what kind of return you need. Should all your assets have the same level of risk? My answer is no. You could say I'm moderately aggressive. But that doesn't mean being moderately aggressive is good for every investment. In a rounded portfolio, some things might be aggressive, some moderate, and some conservative.

If you are worried about your retirement, I hope you will continue to turn these pages. I want you to see what is most likely to work for you. The style of investment that you used to accumulate your savings is unlikely to serve you well now. You might be all right, but you need to know the right questions to ask. You are entering a new world with new rules and risks.

ANSWERING ONLY TO THE CLIENT

I have tailored my practice to focus exclusively on retirement income planning. I only work with retirees or those who are in what is known as the "retirement red zone"—that is, within a decade of taking that step.

I have been in the financial services industry since 1998, and I founded Peterson Financial Group in 2001. My practice is in Des Moines, Iowa, though I was raised in San Diego, California. Some might wonder whether I had a lobotomy to make such a move, and though I do vouch for San Diego's weather advantage, I like the Midwest. It's where my wife grew up. We moved our young family here in 1995.

I got into the financial services industry by working in the home offices of two of the largest, most successful insurance companies in the country, Principal Financial Group and

Equitable Life of Iowa. It was at those firms that I learned from the inside how things work.

But I also realized at that point that no one company has the best of anything. If you work specifically for a company, you're only able to offer that company's products or solutions. I knew if I ever went into my own practice, I would be independent. That's why it's my name on the door today, not that of a big financial services company. I don't answer to anybody but my clients.

FOUR CRUCIAL STEPS

When a new client comes to us, we go through a four-step evaluation that touches on the primary concerns that people face at this stage of life. We do a tax return review, an income analysis, a risk and fee analysis, and an estate plan review. I'll discuss each of those in later chapters, but in short, this is what they entail:

4-STEP EVALUATION

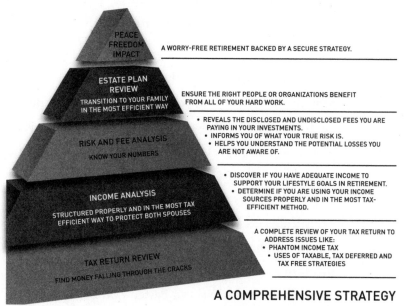

PEACE FREEDOM IMPACT — A WORRY-FREE RETIREMENT BACKED BY A SECURE STRATEGY.

ESTATE PLAN REVIEW
TRANSITION TO YOUR FAMILY IN THE MOST EFFICIENT WAY — ENSURE THE RIGHT PEOPLE OR ORGANIZATIONS BENEFIT FROM ALL OF YOUR HARD WORK.

RISK AND FEE ANALYSIS
KNOW YOUR NUMBERS
- REVEALS THE DISCLOSED AND UNDISCLOSED FEES YOU ARE PAYING IN YOUR INVESTMENTS.
- INFORMS YOU OF WHAT YOUR TRUE RISK IS.
- HELPS YOU UNDERSTAND THE POTENTIAL LOSSES YOU ARE NOT AWARE OF.

INCOME ANALYSIS
STRUCTURED PROPERLY AND IN THE MOST TAX EFFICIENT WAY TO PROTECT BOTH SPOUSES
- DISCOVER IF YOU HAVE ADEQUATE INCOME TO SUPPORT YOUR LIFESTYLE GOALS IN RETIREMENT.
- DETERMINE IF YOU ARE USING YOUR INCOME SOURCES PROPERLY AND IN THE MOST TAX-EFFICIENT METHOD.

TAX RETURN REVIEW
FIND MONEY FALLING THROUGH THE CRACKS
A COMPLETE REVIEW OF YOUR TAX RETURN TO ADDRESS ISSUES LIKE:
- PHANTOM INCOME TAX
- USES OF TAXABLE, TAX DEFERRED AND TAX FREE STRATEGIES

A COMPREHENSIVE STRATEGY

- The tax return review reveals where money may be falling through the cracks. We look at the way you hold investments, what you could be deducting, and whether you are paying tax on income you are not spending. Most of the time, we can save clients hundreds, if not thousands, of dollars in taxes just by examining the way they hold or title their accounts.

- The income analysis is multifaceted but easy to understand. The idea is to structure the income flow properly and in the most tax-efficient way to protect both spouses, and it addresses that fundamental fear: "Will we have enough money to last us for the rest of our lives?" This requires budgeting for immediate, intermediate, and long-term expenditures and investing appropriately so your money lasts. For a couple, that means for both of you. If you stood up, once, in front of God and everyone and vowed to love, honor, and protect your spouse, you want to do so even when you are gone.

- The market risk and fee analysis reveals the costs you face with the investments in your portfolio. Most people are amazed to find out how much they actually are paying. The analysis projects what would happen to your portfolio in various scenarios. For example, if you had a bad year, such as 2008, we can graph those projections statistically, showing the return on your portfolio, the return for the average investor, and how much risk is involved in attaining those results. The graph comes out as a bell curve, and we can flatten that bell and cut off the ends so that you have a more consistent projection of returns for your account.

- The estate plan review looks at the money that you won't be spending in your lifetime. In essence, the issue here is how much of that money you want to go to the IRS, how much you want to go to your family, and how much you want to leave to a charity or a cause. Once you get to the point where you feel reassured, you will be all right financially. Once you are set for life, you begin weighing who will benefit from your life's work. It is important to do so in the right way so that less goes to taxes. It's a matter of your legacy: How can you best benefit the people and institutions that you care most about?

As you can see in the pyramid chart, those steps, done correctly, are topped by "peace, freedom, and impact." You can have the peace of mind of knowing that you have a plan, a structure in place for the most important phase of your life. You will have freedom from worry so that you can enjoy what you want to do. And your life will have an impact on what matters most to you. Why were we put here? What is our purpose? Such questions loom ever larger for many people as they advance into retirement. They begin to ponder posterity.

A PLAN TAILORED FOR YOU

This evaluation culminates in a written investment plan. You get a detailed analysis. All of this is presented to you in an easy-to-understand binder. It's a road map to get you to your chosen destination. And it starts with discovering and identifying that destination: your true needs and desires and goals. Only after that does it make sense to choose investment tools and products. Once you see where you are and where you want to go, you can chart the course to get there and choose the best way to travel.

I believe it is essential that we go through this process before we even start talking about investments. That's how our firm is different from most. We're income-oriented. We believe in setting the foundation, through analysis and budgeting, and establishing your life goals before choosing the pieces for your plan. Most financial firms don't take their clients through such a thorough process. Generally, their conversations go like this: "How much do you have, and who is managing it? We can do much better than *that*." It amounts to "Their stuff stinks; our stuff is better."

We don't assume, upon meeting you, that your investments aren't working. But you can't know until you go through the process to discover *how* they work for you, from all the standpoints. Are they tax-efficient? Are the fees and the market risk reasonable for your circumstances? Do your investments provide you with a reliable income? We start by giving you a foundation and education.

Our approach is based on math, not markets. We can show you what you need mathematically. If you need X amount of income, you will need to deposit Y amount of money. And those figures will work for you regardless of what happens to the markets. It isn't a matter of just hoping things work out. We take guessing out of the income equation by calculating: "If you put in this amount of money, this is the income that will be there for you."

In essence, we tailor a plan just for you. It might be far different from the financial advice you hear on the news or read in the journals or from some talking head who doesn't know beans about your personal situation. We listen carefully to your concerns and needs and directions and goals, and then we custom design. Each of us has unique dreams, values, and tolerance for risk. By getting to know you, we can see whether your portfolio is in alignment with your goals and realistic for retirement.

LET'S GET STARTED

In the chapters ahead, I'll take you on a tour of what good retirement planning is all about. I'll show you how you can breathe free with an income plan designed to make sure that you will have enough to last a lifetime. I'll show you how that works.

We'll take a close look at the Social Security system: Will the benefit be reliable for people retiring today? Will it be there for their children? Should you claim the benefit at 62 or wait several years?

And I'll address other concerns: inflation, taxes, hidden fees in mutual funds, health-care and long-term-care costs, and other threats to one's wealth. These are the issues that weigh on retirees' minds.

With a good retirement plan, you can move forward with confidence, free of debilitating fear, so that you and your heirs might make the most of your life savings. I'll also have some practical advice for you on estate planning.

Rest assured. I am on your side. I act in my clients' best interest. My focus is to help them manage their risk, balancing the need to protect their life savings with the need to grow their assets to beat inflation and share the bounty with generations to come.

At the 2014 Masters Tournament, Bubba Watson was up by two strokes on his closest opponent when he went into the final hole. During the entire tournament, Bubba was outdriving everyone else, using his driver club. It gives players the most distance off the tee, but it also carries the most risk. Bubba Watson chose to use a three-wood off the tee on the final hole, even though he had not gotten into trouble with his driver the entire tournament. Why did he do this? He was already in a position to win the tournament and didn't need to risk losing his position.

The difference between first and second place was close to $1 million. Sometimes, when the game is already won, you need to focus on preserving the win that you have. *Retirement planning and the game of golf have similar fundamentals.* The front nine in golf is comparable to the accumulation phase of retirement planning. You take more chances and play more aggressively because you have the opportunity to improve your score. The back nine is comparable to the preservation and distribution phase in retirement planning. On the back nine, you can't afford the same mistakes that you might have made on the front nine. If you keep playing aggressively, you could lose what you have earned.

CHAPTER ONE

Across the Threshold

"Eric, it hasn't been hard to save and invest, and accumulating money has been easy for us," the new client told me. "What's harder for us now is adjusting to thinking about spending it."

He was a sales professional, and after he and his wife had raised a family, she had worked a bit as a receptionist. The company that he worked for did not provide a traditional pension plan. They did give a very attractive match to his 401(k), and he had accumulated a significant amount of money in it.

They took a big hit in 2008 when he was in his midfifties and hadn't given a thought to retiring yet.

Most of the wealth was in the 401(k), and he wasn't happy about seeing the balance fall, but it wasn't anything that he needed. He wasn't petrified because he figured it would bounce back, as markets do. But he was a little worried about how fast it went down and that everything went down. It wasn't just his stock funds. It was also his bond funds and his REITs (real estate investment trusts).

We went through our review process. They had been unaware of some of the tools available that could replicate a pension for them. We were able to craft a strategy for them, and they were able to have all the income they wanted, coming from a guaranteed source that would last them the rest of their lifetimes.

It didn't take nearly as much money as they had anticipated, only about 35 percent of the value that they had accumulated. The rest of the money was then earmarked or set aside for growth to help combat inflation and to provide a legacy. They wanted to leave money to their kids and grandkids.

We were able to predict exactly what their retirement income would be when they retired in several years. What we try to solve is the gap. Going through a budget process, we figured out how much they required in retirement income beyond the Social Security benefit and how much it would take of their personal savings to fill that gap. The goal is to use guaranteed sources to meet their monthly obligations in retirement.

A NEW CONFIDENCE

That couple will be just fine. They were scared in the beginning, but now they have a new confidence. They know that regardless of what the market will do, they're going to be okay.

Unfortunately, many scared people have remained that way. They are still following their broker's advice to just hang in there. They don't explore alternatives that can help them have peace of mind. They go into retirement worried, because they know that their nest egg is fragile.

The market can only do one of three things: It can go up, it can go down, or it can go sideways. Unfortunately, most people saving for retirement are investing in the traditional model that works only when the market is going up. For our clients, we create retirement income plans that will work in any scenario. That is what instills confidence.

WHICH WAY IS THE MARKET GOING?

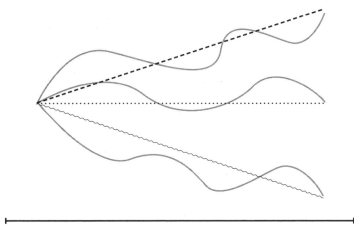

The Next Several Years

You need to have all elements of the investment world at your disposal in retirement. It is important to plan a reliable income that takes into consideration when you need the money and for what purpose. I'll go into detail about that later in this book.

MIXED EXPECTATIONS

People often launch into retirement with a vision of what life will be like for them now. Perhaps they feel they will be sitting back to relax, but when that turns out to be boring, they look for things to do and find themselves busier than ever and wondering how they ever had time for a job. Others have no choice but to take a job to pay the bills.

When I ask people what their vision of retirement is, traveling is high on the list. I hear "visiting the grandkids" a lot. Among professionals, particularly, the desire to volunteer and give back is a common response.

As for me, I would want to enjoy my family, travel with my wife, relax on a cruise, or enjoy a glass of wine while watching the sunset in some exotic and balmy clime. My vision of retirement is not watching CNBC every day. It's not logging into my accounts and making trades. It's not watching the ticker at the bottom of a news channel screen to see whether any of my wealth evaporated at the closing bell.

A TROUBLING TIME FOR MANY

Vast numbers of people will retire in the years ahead as the baby boomers age. Each day, 10,000 people turn 65 years of age, and we've only just begun. It's like the pig in the python. The baby boom has been working its way through society. It worked its way through the maternity wards, the school systems and colleges, and the workforce. The boomers became consumers and home buyers and investors, and now they are becoming retirees.

That demographic wave changes everything it touches. It will continue to influence the need for health care and further shock the already suffering Social Security system. It is a force for momentous change in society, and that force now is getting very gray, and many are having difficulty adjusting.

This new phase of life can be as troubling as it is delightful. Some suffer from the loss of their work identity. I see that particularly in people who had one job their entire working lives.

I knew a man who worked at a local company here for 47 years, often putting in 12-hour days. His whole identity was with his job. He installed a shower in the basement of his home so as not to disturb his family when he got up early to go to work. He'd get there before dawn and work until evening. Once home, he was out as soon as he sat down on the couch. And then he retired. But he really had no plan for how to retire. He didn't know what to do with himself. Within a few years, he was dead.

People spend more of their waking hours at work than they do at home. They often are more connected to coworkers than to family. And when those connections are taken away, what then? Something needs to fill that time and replace those relationships, as well as replace the income. "When somebody retires," the joke goes, "the wife gets 100 percent of the husband and half the income."

Retirement should be joyful, but it also takes a lot of adjustment. There are new rules. It helps to work with someone who can assist you in planning for a future, not just figuring out where to put your money but how to make it work in concert with your goals. There are so many facets to retirement planning. It's not just about money, though money and a reliable income are an integral part of it as a means to reach for those goals.

Fulfillment doesn't come from money. Money helps advance the goals that you've set for yourself, and that is why you need to focus on rounding out your life. You're unlikely to be happy watching television all day. A lot of people still need to feel productive. They want to know that they are contributing and improving society, and they can do that in a wide variety of ways.

A NEW PERSPECTIVE

If you are retired or closing in on retirement age, I'm sure you can easily reflect on how much the concerns of life have changed. You may recall the day you bought your own house, probably at a double-digit interest rate. For $25, you could fill the back seat of your car with groceries—that is, if there was any room once the kids were buckled in. Your focus in life was on establishing yourself, getting those promotions and pay raises, starting and raising a family, and perhaps, getting the kids off to college. You wondered how you ever would afford it all, but somehow you got through.

Retirement was some far-off place then. When you were in your twenties and thirties, it may have been hard to think seriously about it. When you did, you imagined a time when you would have the money to do whatever you wanted. You saw yourself as an older version of yourself with boundless energy. Maybe your retirement would be spent forever at the beach. You've yet to feel many of the aches and pains of body and life.

Then, that perspective shifts. By your midforties, thoughts of retirement keep crowding in. Your antenna goes up as you realize you are only 15 or 20 years away from it, particularly if you dream of retiring early.

You sense, in other words, that time is not as endless as it once seemed. When you are young, your biggest asset is time. You look at your portfolio, and you see years stretching ahead for your investments to work their magic. Successful investing requires that you have either a lot of time or a lot of money. If you have a lot of time, the money will build. If you don't have a lot of time, you need a lot of money.

You may not have understood the term *dollar-cost averaging* when you were starting out, but you engaged in it nonetheless if you set money aside regularly for the future in an account that you tried not to touch—say, a 401(k) invested in a package of equities. Every other week, or every month, you bought into your investments whether the market was up or down. If the market was down, you bought on sale, and of course, as the market rose, your portfolio rose with it.

Such steady contributions take advantage of the movements of the market. But, in retirement, that perspective changes if you now have to withdraw money from that fluctuating account for your income. In a down market, you aren't buying things on sale. Instead, you are forced to sell at a sale price for someone else, and that illustrates one of the dramatic changes in perspective encountered in retirement.

THE CHALLENGES ARE CHANGING

Retirement is a new world of challenges. Some involve pressures that have been there all along, such as inflation and taxes, but they take on new dimensions now. Others are simply a matter of uncertainty: How long will you live and need an income? What financial surprises or emergencies might come your way? How will your health hold out?

When you were getting those promotions and pay raises during your accumulation years, you may not have been all that concerned about inflation. The raises kept pace. Now, in retirement, inflation becomes another of your worries; or, at least, it should. You are probably on a fixed income. You cannot simply project how well you will be doing in the years ahead based on the current income you can produce. You need to factor in the role of inflation, and at its historical levels, not at the tamer rate of recent years.

Many retirees are frankly fearful that they will run out of money before they die. When the AARP did a survey of fears, that one ranked higher than death and public speaking. When you run out of money in retirement, you run out of options.

Those concerns have been accentuated in recent years as people have seen firsthand what can happen. They've seen how a market can devastate their money. They've heard about, or witnessed, or maybe experienced, the financial crush of a health-care crisis. Without proper planning, people can lose their life savings.

People actually fear their own potential for longevity. It's the flip side of the primal fear of death. All in all, believe it or not, we are getting healthier. Medical advances keep us around a lot longer. In Chapter 8, we'll talk in more detail about the need to plan for a health-care emergency and the fact that you're going to be old and frail someday. That can take quite a toll on your portfolio.

A lot of other things are swirling around in the head of a typical retiree. People have seen, for example, what taxes can do. All through their life they've struggled with how to manage taxes, and they worry that they're not going to manage them properly or lose too much to the government and not have enough left for their heirs.

Most people, during the course of their lives, try to save up money for an emergency. They know that they well could have a sudden need. The money in that fund needs to be liquid. In other words, can they get easy access without penalty? Retirees also worry about whether they will be able to help their children and grandkids. They want to have the resources to play an effective role in their lives.

ENTERING THE PRESERVATION STAGE

In retirement, you have entered the preservation stage of life. You've accumulated the assets, and now you need to start protecting what you have and make it last. The focus is not really on accumulation anymore. It's now on spending and preserving it—the distribution and preservation stage.

The thing to ask yourself at this stage of life, and the question I ask retirees is "If the money you have were to double tomorrow, is that going to change your lifestyle?" Everyone says, "No, it won't change my lifestyle." Then, I ask them, "If the amount of money that you have were to go down by half, if you were to lose half of your money, would that affect you?" and the answer always is yes.

At this stage in life, if doubling your money is not going to change what you do, but losing half of it would, you want to explore strategies that will help reduce or eliminate the risk of losing what you have accumulated.

The focus needs to change. The whole reason you invest and take risk, or start a business and take risk, is to make money. Once you've done so and you have reached the point of retirement, you should no longer focus on accumulating money. You should focus on protecting it and using your savings to generate cash flow to pay yourself back.

In general, protecting your life savings means subjecting it to less market risk, although you probably won't want to avoid risk in every component of your portfolio. You do need adequate growth. In Chapter 9, on planning an income for retirement, I will go into detail about the three worlds of money: the world of safety, the world of growth, and a newer "linked" world that combines elements of both.

In short, your income plan will need to visit all of those worlds, depending on when and how you intend to use the money. You will need to keep some of your money safe to meet your more immediate needs and goals, but other money that you won't need for a while you can invest to earn a higher rate. That will be important if you are to keep up with inflation and build a reserve for later years of your retirement. The "linked" world, as we will see, offers safety, but with a better return than you might otherwise expect.

SO MANY THREATS

In the preservation stage of life, investments should have less risk. You do have to pay attention to inflation, so you still need to have assets growing. The Wall Street firms often suggest that inflation is the only risk that is out there. It's not. There are all kinds of risks out there, and inflation is just one of them.

Let's say inflation is 3 percent. Do you beat it by taking a risk and losing 30 percent of your money? To me, that's no way to beat inflation. It's easier to beat inflation if all you have to do is come up with that 3 percent. In other words, if your basic needs are met—that is, needs you'll always have, regardless of what happens to the markets—you have this guaranteed cash flow. If inflation hits, you just go to your other assets and take out a little bit.

As you can see, the market can pose a greater risk than inflation if you expose too much of your portfolio to it. You need to protect your assets because a host of other risks could be lying in wait. Good planning anticipates those risks and contingencies. To name some others: a serious or prolonged illness, particularly if it requires nursing home care; the death of a spouse, which could eliminate a source of pension or other income; and divorce, for which the rate among retirees is high.

GETTING READY FOR THE CHANGE

Once you decide to retire, this shift from accumulation thinking to preservation and distribution should not take place suddenly, as if you were flipping a switch. There are some things you can do to prepare while you're in the world of accumulation. The two phases overlap.

Life's exigencies can make it necessary to start thinking about preserving your money much earlier than you might think. At any age, a life event such as the death of a spouse or the loss of a job might call for a change in strategies. You always should have a safety net, no matter how old you are. With advance preparation, the transition is much smoother.

Through the types of tools and planning that we can offer, you can have distribution-type accounts in accumulation mode. They're just waiting and building. Let's say you are 55 years old and 10 years away from retirement. Mathematically, I can say if you want $1,000 a month of income at age 65 for you and your spouse, you would have to put in approximately $110,000 today. That would be at a 5 percent interest rate that you could earn regardless of what happens to the market or economy.

That's the beauty of the types of tools that are now available for today's retirees if they choose to avail themselves of them. As you get closer to retirement, there's a lot of wisdom in choosing certainty.

NO RETIREE IS AN ISLAND

Let me reassure you that so many others share the concerns you may be facing now. Your individual needs are unique, of course, but you are not alone. Someone else has faced a similar scenario, and I have seen a wide variety of what retirees encounter.

Some have more savings and investments than others do but no pension. Some have secure pensions but have saved relatively little. The variables differ, but it is certain that in retirement we all will need a continuing income that is adequate to support our lifestyle. We get up, turn on the lights, eat breakfast, take our medicine, run errands and shop, and take trips. As we keep on living, we keep on incurring expenses. We need an income. The difference is the source.

Think of yourself and your family as a company. You are in charge of deploying your accumulated assets so that the company—that is, your family—can do well when going into the new phase. You are the CEO, and you are responsible for the assets of your company. As with any company, some of those assets will produce income for salary. Some of those assets can be reinvested to grow the business. The goal of this company is to provide a success-ful retirement, which also means an enjoyable and fulfilling one. Otherwise, what's the point? What is the purpose of a company unless it provides for a better and happier life?

Good leaders, whether of a business or of a family, find the right people for the tasks at hand. Investment is one of those tasks that responsible people often delegate while they attend to the big picture. That doesn't mean you must do none of your own investing, if that's what you enjoy. I have clients who keep a piece of the action for themselves. They want to be able to pick their own stocks. It gets their juices flowing, but if they are going to take a risk with that portion, they need to have guarantees in place for other investments and a steady stream of income. Only then should they have the confidence to gamble.

I recognize that some clients have great ideas on investing. I applaud that. I want to be there to guide them through the big picture and to show them things they might not have considered outside their current box of knowledge.

As you cross the threshold into retirement, know that legions of others have crossed before you. You do not stand alone. Wisdom comes by way of learning from the experiences of others and that amounts to a great wealth of information. It is time to focus on living as well as you can from what you have set aside for this extraordinary time of life.

CHAPTER TWO

Climbing the Pyramid

The couple came in with grandiose ideas about what they were going to be able to do in retirement. And what they planned to do involved a lot of spending, as they were currently doing, keeping up with the expenses of maintaining a large house.

They were in their early fifties at the time and weren't saving a lot. Nonetheless, the husband told me that, come age 60, he was going to retire early. He figured he would do a reverse mortgage at age 62, get the full value of his house, buy a little place to live, and have money left over to supplement the retirement years and enjoy life.

The man was stunned to learn that reverse mortgages don't deliver 100 percent of the value of a home. The maximum he could get would be 40 or 50 percent, and that's when he realized that their retirement dreams were not in line with the resources he was committing.

I worked with that couple on a switch in strategies. For one, they had to immediately begin to spend less and save more. The good news was that he was young enough to correct their trajectory. We were able to demonstrate ways to grow their money in a more conservative way. We were able to place some guarantees in their account that would grow at a rate that was faster than they were getting on other investments.

They also had to realize that retirement at age 60 was probably not going to be in the cards for them. They would probably have to work until they were 65 or 66. They found out what they needed well enough in advance to do something about it. Some people don't. That can lead to real problems and deep disappointments—and a substantial change in the quality of life they had expected.

NO MAGIC WAND

One of my favorite cartoons—shown below—depicts a client visiting a financial planner.

© Randy Glasbergen / glasbergen.com

**Investments and
Financial Planning**

GLASBERGEN

"I retire on Friday and I haven't saved a dime.
Here's your chance to become a legend!"

Some people think that retirement planners have some kind of magic wand that can turn their resources into more than what they are. Instead, it's really a simple formula: spend below what you have coming in.

On the bright side, however, people often find that they have a lot more resources than they think they have. They find that they have been worrying unnecessarily.

I worked with another couple who both were fortunate enough to have pensions. Nonetheless, during the interview, she expressed her fear that she was going to end up a bag lady. She worried that if her husband were to die, she would be on the street.

"I just want enough money to be able to afford a couple of apples," she said.

They had never gone through a planning process. Together, we went through their budget and what they were actually spending. We found that with their pension and Social Security benefit, their income was double their expenses. They had a tremendous amount in savings.

During their years together, they had done without a lot to save as much as they did. And now, at the dawn of retirement, they were scared to enjoy it. They feared being penniless. What they really lacked was confidence.

It's sad to never get to that level of confidence where you know you will be all right. Even though some people see that their numbers all work out, they continue to live so frugally that they pass up memories they could have made. Life's most enjoyable years can come in retirement if you let them. Some don't let them, because they simply don't know what they have.

That underscores the dual need for effective retirement planning. You need advance warning if things aren't all right, certainly, but you also need reassurance that you should be doing just fine.

SO WHAT'S NEXT IN LIFE?

This is the time of life when people begin to think of what they have always wanted to do, what they will leave behind, and how they will be remembered. Until you know your goals and priorities, you can't create an effective retirement plan. You can't plan until you know what you want to do.

If you're going to go on a trip, you don't just get in the car and say, "Hey, let's see where this road takes us." You plan out your journey, the stops along the way, and the interesting things that you want to see.

A lot of people don't treat retirement like that. They just think of it as getting to a point where they'll have the money to retire, and from there, they'll just live. They don't have a structure or think about what it takes for them to live or what they really want to do. A lot of people reach retirement and feel that something is missing, so they want to go back to work.

You need to contemplate your vision. It's not just the finances. Think about other things you want to do: hobbies, getting more active in the community, volunteering, church, and grandkids. You need to think about what it is you want to do in retirement and build your resources around that.

The recession of 2008–2009 rocked a lot of people's foundations. They lost their dreams. That's why they don't really have concrete visions any more. They saw what that market did. On the cusp of retirement, some people lost 35 to 40 percent of their retirement nest egg.

And some have remained shell-shocked. Perhaps they missed the rebound. It's high time that they start to plan effectively. But to do so, they have to know what they see as their future. Financial planners can help clients best if they have a vision of what their clients want to do. That way, the vision can be compared with the resources, and the starting point for the journey can be seen.

A good trip requires organizing, and that means more than organizing documents, although that, too, as we will see, is critical. Your life priorities need to be in order.

Do you want to do much traveling, and if so, where? Do you want to visit the grandkids or go to distant lands? Retirees often can get vacation deals more readily because of their greater flexibility in travel time. Or they can drive and save on some expenses, sightseeing along the way. Vacation during retirement is a lot different from vacation during the working years. While you were working, you wanted to get the maximum amount of fun in the shortest amount of time. In retirement, part of the fun is the journey along the way. You can take your time to savor it and enjoy it.

Who matters to you? What organizations and causes would you like to support? Why are you here? What do you care about? What's important to you? Whom do you want to help? What kind of things do you want to learn? Those are the kinds of questions to ask, and the answers will have a lot to do with how you spend and what becomes of your money.

Some people want to pursue degrees. They want to take classes in photography or art, perhaps. Education is a lifelong endeavor. One of the fastest growing segments in community colleges is adult education, and it can be at little cost. Here, in the Des Moines area, the community college has a 36-page catalog full of adult education classes, including automotive, finance, pottery, and much more. I'm sure that reflects the aging of the population.

You should plan what you want to have happen. So many people don't take the time to do that. Retirement should be fun. Retirees remain active, with active and creative minds. They have so much that they want to do. You shouldn't enter retirement full of worry and despair. You should be looking forward to this time.

PATTERNS OF SPENDING

In the years I have been specializing in working with retirees, I have seen patterns. Retirees tend to spend less the older they get.

When you first reach retirement, you are gung ho; there are a lot of things that you'll do, not only traveling but also making improvements to your home. You do the things you always wanted to get done because, now, you have the time. Some retirees actually get their home ready for retirement. A lot of people, anticipating health problems, will move furnishings around so everything is on one level and they don't have to negotiate stairs as much. Or maybe they move into a home where they don't have responsibility for the exterior maintenance anymore, such as mowing the lawns and shoveling snow.

Expenses tend to be higher during the first five to ten years of retirement. After that, traveling is likely to become more regional than international or even national. Enjoyment may be found in simpler things. Expenses tend to better match income. A lot of times, what is coming in isn't spent, in which case, retirement money increases.

In the planning process, we can adjust for that change in lifestyle. Typically, in an estate plan or in a retirement plan, we're going to assume a level of expense. We're going to run with those expenses throughout the entire retirement income plan to make sure it works. We stress test it under those conditions.

People tend to look at their gross income as opposed to their net income. If you make $100,000 a year but put $20,000 into your 401(k) and pay $20,000 in taxes, you have $60,000 remaining. That's what you have been living on. But people compute their retirement needs as 80 percent of the gross, which in that example is $80,000. That's when they get scared. It looks as if their retirement plan won't work. But, more accurately, they need 80 percent of the $60,000, or $48,000.

That's why the first step in creating a plan is going through the budget process to determine what you will spend in retirement. You need to find out whether your goals and dreams are as realistic as the numbers show. If you plan to go on a cruise around the world and stay at the Ritz-Carlton in Paris for six weeks out of the year, your plan may be unrealistic. If you are going to dream the impossible dream, you should at least know it's unrealistic.

ORGANIZING DOCUMENTS

As you organize your life and goals, you also have to organize your documents and statements. You need to keep track of where the money is and the steps you have taken. If something were to happen to both you and your spouse, would your kids or your heirs be able to access your information and take action on your behalf? If not, you need to organize your documentation so they can do so.

We give clients a binder containing all their documents and an organizer for phone numbers, account numbers, and other essential and useful information. You want the people you care about to be able to work smoothly toward the goals you have set forth.

You should keep your files someplace secure. A fireproof safe in the house is, of course, best. If you don't have a fireproof safe, consider putting the most important documents in a heavy-duty plastic bag and storing them in the freezer, which also tends to be fireproof.

You should discuss these matters at a family meeting. It's not much fun to talk about with the kids, but you want to educate them on where you keep your documents, and let them know whom you have entrusted with financial matters, such as your CPA, attorney, and financial advisor, and how to contact them. You might want to introduce them in person. That can take a level of stress off your loved ones so that they aren't dealing with total strangers upon your passing.

At minimum, you should have a will, a living will if you do not wish to be kept alive by artificial means; powers of attorney for finances and health care, which you will not be able to grant once you are incapacitated; and a living trust if you want to avoid the delay, costs, and problems of probate.

If you have children with special needs, you might also want to consider a trust. I'm not an attorney, but I do know the power of those documents and often refer my clients to an attorney who can help get that done.

THE DANGERS OF DELAYING

It can indeed seem an overwhelming task to take care of all these things, but if you procrastinate, any problems are likely to get bigger. I understand why people wait. It's easy to put things off. I keep saying I will work on the basement next month, or next year, until I feel like throwing up my hands, wondering if I'll ever get it done. A task can seem insurmountable, but as the old saying goes, how do you eat an elephant? One bite at a time. It's easy to procrastinate, because it's hard to deal with matters of life and death. You are looking into the future when you will be old and facing some difficult issues. It's not fun.

Some people suggest that you plan your funeral. That isn't exactly uplifting either, but it relieves your loved ones of a huge burden. Planning your funeral is not necessarily morbid; it's telling the people you care about how you want things to be: how you will be dressed, the flowers, the music. Also, there are ways to cover those expenses for your heirs. Funeral planning is the loving thing to do. It shows deep care for the people who will be left behind.

One very practical reason to avoid procrastination is that it could cost your surviving spouse the money you intended for him or her. You need to go over your documents to see who the beneficiaries are.

Otherwise, there could be some very nasty surprises.

CPA and IRA guru Ed Slott often relates the story of a couple who married later in life. She worked for the school system, and he worked for parks and recreation. When she died, he found out that the beneficiaries designated in her 403(b) retirement plan were her mother, uncle, and sister. The benefit was worth $1 million. Her mother and uncle had already passed away. Her sister could have disclaimed it. But she didn't. The case went all the way to the New York Supreme Court, and he lost. The justices said the beneficiary designation was the rule. The sister got a million-dollar plan, of which she gave her brother-in-law not a cent, and he got a greatly reduced lifestyle.

CLIMBING TO YOUR GOALS

Our four-step review process—taxes, income, market risk and fees, estate—is a good guide along the journey to retirement, but you need to know where you are going. You need to know what you want out of your retirement. Otherwise, those steps will lack the necessary context to be meaningful.

You might think of your retirement plan as a pyramid that you progressively climb from the foundational stones to the pinnacle, where you reach the ultimate goals: the peace of mind from knowing you will have the retirement you've dreamed about; the freedom to enjoy it; and a lasting impact on those you care about, whether your family or your community.

Once you have achieved those things, once you have made it to the pinnacle, your retirement can be blissful and free of stress. You have built a sturdy foundation from which you have been able to see all the way to the top, with secure footholds along the way.

CHAPTER THREE

Who Has Your Back?

The husband didn't have much to say at first. He and his wife had come in to begin retirement planning, but he sat mostly in silence, looking uneasy. He seemed jaded.

"Let me ask you," I said, "how you would answer the question, 'what does money mean to you?'"

And then he started to open up. He told me of an impoverished childhood in which there never seemed to be enough money even for basic needs. He shared the details of a long struggle. His demeanor softened as he spoke, as if he felt relieved that he could tell me this. His wife began to cry.

It is important for us to find out how people view money. That's why we engage in the type of planning that we do. We know how hard our clients have worked for their money, sometimes against great odds. We are there to help them protect it.

Those who have been through hard times will feel that need with particular urgency. Deep inside, no matter how well they have done, they fear returning to that sad state. The voice inside them has long chanted, "Don't lose your money. Don't lose your money." It remains fundamental to how some people think about money, and a good financial advisor must be sensitive to such feelings.

Each of us, early in life, forms an attitude toward money that remains for a lifetime. When we understand how clients feel about money, we know which tools or services are going to best suit them and their mentality. They can gain the confidence to enjoy this most precious time of their life. We can stress-test the financial plan so they see how they would fare even in the worst-case scenario of a bad economic market. By seeing they will be all right, they feel deeply relieved. They see that we have their back.

TAPPING INTO EMOTIONS

Financial advising often taps into emotions that may have gone unexpressed for years. That can happen particularly when a couple begins to talk about issues involving their children and who should inherit what. Spouses often sharply disagree. This may be the first time that couples have openly discussed issues involving their future. I'll ask both the husband and the wife, in turn, about their thoughts on a matter, and a lot of times, they are not aligned at all. The husband looks at the wife and says, "I never knew that," and she says, "Well, you never asked."

The emotions can also run high because people tend to come to us during times of crisis, either in the economy or in their personal lives. We tend to get busier the worse the markets do, because it drives home the fact that the economy isn't always bright. People see the real potential for loss and the need for protection, and they appeal to us for help.

Sometimes the tears are tears of relief instead of the tears of fear. A wife may be imagining how she will endure if her husband is no longer there to provide or handle the finances. Often she will see, once we run the numbers, that she will be just fine. She needs reassurance.

We can look a husband in the eye and say, "If something happens to you, your wife is going to be okay." We see many couples in traditional family roles in which the husband is the provider and handles the finances. Statistically, the husband will die first. The widow wants to know there will be money to pay the bills and put food on the table and maybe take a trip or two and visit the grandkids. That's what concerns her, whether or not she knows how financial instruments work.

That's where the services of a specialist are more important than ever. Most people, when they envision retirement, don't see themselves sitting at a laptop, constantly refreshing the glowing screen to see how their investments are doing. They expect to relax. Isn't that what retirement is all about? They don't want to be stressed out or micromanaging. Unless the intricacies of investment are truly their forte, they should engage reliable and trustworthy professional assistance well in advance.

QUESTIONABLE ADVICE

Bad advice is all around us, whether it comes from stockbrokers, the media, the Internet, or well-meaning friends.

In the traditional Wall Street model, brokers were only compensated based on transactions. It didn't really matter, from their perspective, whether an account went up, because their fees were derived solely from buying and selling. That's how the industry started. When the broker called to warn a client that a particular stock was a dog, that client well might be exchanging one dog for another. The brokers just knew they got a commission every time their clients bought. They needed a lot of churn, a lot of transactions, to generate their own income.

Brokers are really going to operate the same way with you whether you're 35 years old or 65 or 75 years old. They're not thinking about your changing needs as much as they should. They want to control the money. They want to keep you in a pen, like a cow, so that they can milk you.

Not all advisors, as you can see, are created equal. Consider whether your advisor earns his or her pay from commissions on transactions or from a fee on your account.

Commissions aren't bad, in and of themselves. They are an incentive to work hard. Those who sell more can make more. What's bad is when you have repetitious buying and selling inside your account for the sole purpose of generating commissions.

If the product and strategy fits your plan, a commission isn't a bad thing. Our society has placed a negative connotation on commissions that suggests those earning them are only looking out for their own interests and not their clients'. But some valuable financial tools provide guarantees for a retiree's income plan, and they generate commissions. That's the way the industry was set up decades ago. A tool should not be rejected just because it generates a commission.

What is most important is that the client's individual goals are accomplished. That's not going to happen with the advice given in the mass media, where people often go for financial advice. They watch the talking heads on television. They read the financial magazines. If you watch any of the popular investing shows, understand the difference between a trader and a saver. Most of the shows are geared toward the trader, who makes daily moves. But if you are a retirement saver, your perspective is long-term. Such shows could lead you to second-guess every little thing. You could end up comparing yourself to the Joneses. You hear people talk about how much money they made on a trade, and you wonder why you didn't make that. That mindset easily can hurt you. That's why it's better to stick to a concrete plan.

It's kind of like gambling. You have to remember that the investment guru on CNBC might be sitting there with $1 billion. When you have $1 billion, you can take risks. If you lose half your investment, you still have $500 million. If your portfolio is only a few hundred thousand dollars, however, you can't afford to lose half of your investment. That's a serious impact on your income.

You can't do the same things that Warren Buffett can do. You can't take the same risks that T. Boone Pickens can take. Before 2008 he was worth $4 billion. Now he's only worth $1 billion. He lost two of those billions on an investment and the third in the market. Is he worried? No. Why? Because he still has $1 billion. That's more money than he'll be able to spend in his lifetime.

Suppose your retirement nest egg is $1 million. If you lost three-quarters of that, you would surely be deeply concerned about your future. Regardless of how much money you have, things still cost the same. Warren Buffett doesn't pay $10,000 for a gallon of milk to make the price relative. Two individuals, one with a portfolio of $10 million and the other with $1 million, could have the same fixed living expenses.

When it comes to investment advice, one size doesn't fit all. You have to have individualized advice. You're going to get mass-market advice from the media. And beware the Internet. Anyone sitting with a keyboard and an Internet connection can post something without verification. You could be lured into an investment that is not right for you. The Internet does give you access to a wealth of information and ideas, but it can be dangerous to act without consulting someone who cares about you, specifically.

You need advice from somebody who is knowledgeable, who has credentials, extensive experience, and a stellar track record.

You need someone who can help you process the avalanche of information on the Internet, because no one can hope to read through all of it. As I wrote this, I typed "annuity" into the Google search engine and got 4,040,000 hits. If you spent one minute reading each of those results, as a full-time job five days a week, it would take you 32 years to review all of the results on annuities. That gives you quite a perspective.

A lot of people listen religiously to what neighbors or colleagues tell them is the best way to invest.

Again, the problem is that they are not you. They don't have the same perspective or the same needs. Yet people compare themselves to others and want to keep up. But do they really know the others' circumstances?

People tend to talk about their winners and never about their losers. Ask any gambler. Gamblers always tell you how much they won, never how much they lost. And that's the way it is around the water cooler. It might be fun to hear a stock tip, but the smart money goes with the true professionals who are solidly on your side.

FIDUCIARY RESPONSIBILITY

Fiduciaries are held to a stricter standard. They not only have the moral and ethical responsibility to act in the client's best interests but they also have the legal responsibility to do so. Those of us on the advisory side of the investment community have been using the fiduciary standard for years.

The fiduciary standard adds another level of obligation to the client. In the fiduciary world, the standard of care is to do what's best for the client, mainly, always putting the client's interests before the advisor's. It also requires disclosing any possible conflicts of interest, including compensation related to products. A fiduciary firm could be liable for high damages if it were to breach those responsibilities.

It's a higher standard than the "suitability" standard of care, in which the advisor need only provide financial products considered suitable for the client's objectives, income level, and age. No disclosure of possible conflicts of interest is required.

Some firms don't want to be held to that higher fiduciary standard. It's in your best interest to find one that does meet that standard. To whom does the advisor answer? If it's not the advisor's name on the door, and on the stationery, he or she answers to somebody else, and the goals of that organization might not be aligned with your own. Peterson Financial Group is a Registered Investment Advisor and is held to the fiduciary standard.

Besides the standard of fiduciary responsibility, you should look for a number of other qualities when you're choosing an advisor. It's like a marriage. You're going to spend years with this person. You want to make sure it's somebody with whom you're comfortable. You don't want to dread going to your financial advisor. You also want to make sure that you approve of the advisor's methods and core beliefs.

TAILORED TO YOUR NEEDS

A good retirement advisor tailors a plan to meet the client's unique needs and goals. The cookie-cutter approach just won't do any longer, if it ever did. During the accumulation years, standard advice can be helpful because you are trying to grow your money, and you are looking for the best investments to help you grow it.

In the distribution years, your financial plan has to take a close account of your goals, objectives, and assets.

In our practice, we do at least annual reviews after the client is comfortable with the plan and projections. I believe that if you put in a lot of work up front, you shouldn't need to do a lot of tweaking along the way. We put more emphasis on safety and certainty, and therefore you don't need to revisit the plan every quarter. We look at it, usually, once a year, and that allows us to make broader adjustments. We'd rather take the time to set the stage carefully so that bad times don't hurt you. We have professionals who will monitor that for you.

When you've graduated to the world of institutional asset management, neither the advisor nor the client asks, "Do we make a move now and rotate out of stocks to bonds?" That's what the institutional manager is doing. You can concentrate on living and enjoying retirement instead of struggling to manage a portfolio day by day. We evaluate those professionals, usually, on an annual basis.

THE COACH AND THE TEAM

Every good athlete has a coach. As a financial coach, my job is to bring out the best in you. But you have the final say. The client keeps control while gaining an advisor's expertise. People seek help because they want that expertise. They recognize that nobody can know it all.

Sure, you could do almost anything if you put enough time and energy into it. But do you want to still shoulder that responsibility as you enter retirement? Is your vision of retirement to manage your portfolio every day and seek the right distributions and deal with tax issues and coordinate distribution strategies, or would you rather be doing something you enjoy?

The coach isn't the athlete. You're the one with the assets. A good coach has years of experience in making the most of those assets, but you are the one whose talents and skills have brought those assets into play. You have the wealth. The coach has a wealth of knowledge about what works best. He's advising you on what you need to know to truly excel.

You not only have a coach, but you also have a team. I have an office staff. I have assistants who help with paperwork and operations. I have people who handle the scheduling of appointments and who mail out reports and items to clients. I have a person who helps with the marketing and getting us in front of people or scheduling educational events and ways for us to meet people. I have people who help me in crafting the plans.

But it's what's behind me, what people don't see, that is really important. They may see only four or five people in my office. What they don't see is that I have hundreds of thousands of employees who support the work we do and are there to help my clients.

I have all the resources of Fidelity Institutional Wealth Management, whose people and technology help us to protect our clients' money from all the predators out there, including hackers and identity thieves. I have those vast resources to protect my clients. In addition, I have access to attorneys and advanced case consultants to keep me informed about changes in our industry and to help my clients craft the best plans possible. You'll only see a few faces in the office, but we have an army of people behind us, offering support to our clients.

I don't try to do everything. I'm very good at what I do, but I know what I'm not good at, so I bring in people who are better at those things than I am. That, again, is in the spirit of delegation, and any good professional understands its power. It enhances the value of the package of services offered to the client.

FIVE CRITICAL QUESTIONS

It's the questions we don't ask that can cost us dearly. When you are working with a financial representative, the initial questions you should ask are not about the return on the investment. That's the mentality of "fire, ready, aim," which ignores the order of priorities.

Here are five critical questions to ask your advisor before you make a financial decision, especially when it puts your money at risk. I deal with each of these questions in greater detail throughout this book.

- **Have you adequately reviewed my personal financial situation to make sure this recommendation is in my best interest?**

  No advisor can make a sound financial recommendation without reviewing your whole personal situation. If you didn't feel well, would you expect a doctor to just reach right into the medical kit and give you a pill? That's not the kind of doctor you likely would want to see. You should expect thorough questioning and an examination.

- **How will this plan affect my tax return each year, and what future tax issues may concern me?**

  If you look at the statement from any large brokerage or financial firm, you will see this disclaimer in fine print:

"We are not tax advisors." Nonetheless, what they do directly affects your tax return. I did a tax review for a new client and saw a substantial capital gains tax. He had bought a large amount of mutual funds the previous year. Why? "I don't know. My broker told me to do that." We got the broker on the speakerphone and asked if he realized what would happen. "I'm not a tax advisor," he said. "That's not my responsibility." But even though he wasn't a tax advisor, he easily could have recommended that his client consult one. That's not giving tax advice.

- **How will your plan affect my income and liquidity needs in the future?**

   Your money serves you in more than one way. It sounds obvious, but your investments should reflect that truth. Some of your goals come sooner, and some later. For those that come soon, such as paying the bills, you must make sure you have access to that money. In other words, some of your money must be kept liquid and free of risk. Other money can be invested for greater gain, but you won't be able to touch it without penalty, and you might face a market loss. Taking 4 percent annually out of a portfolio is not an income plan. It's simply your withdrawal rate. Perhaps you assume that if you're getting a 6 percent return, you will be just fine. And everything does work great when accounts go up. But they often go down too. If you lose 10 percent and still take out that 4 percent, you have locked in a 14 percent loss. A few years of that devastation, and a millionaire might be going back to work.

- **How does your plan match up with my risk comfort level?**

  People often don't have a good handle on what their risk tolerance actually is. You might get a list of questions that purport to determine that tolerance, and you get a score, and you're told you should fit one model or another with investments suitable for people like you. But in an economic scare, aggressive investors can suddenly become conservative ones. In other words, the answer to questions about risk tolerance is that it depends. It depends on your circumstances, the economy, and your goal for that portion of your money. You can't risk the grocery budget, hoping to generate a bit more cash. But you might be more aggressive with money you won't need for a decade or more.

- **How will your plan affect the transition of my estate to my heirs?**

  Two entities will benefit from your leftover wealth: your family and the IRS. The question is, which one do you want to receive more? You also will want to work with your advisor to look for ways you might help not only your family but also organizations and entities you care about.

Most people's interaction with a new investment advisor goes like this: "What do you have? Where is it? Oh…I can do much better." It's all about the money. Proper retirement planning involves much more discovery, and the conversations should be deeper and focused on getting to know you and what you want to have happen in retirement.

YOUR ADVISOR'S TRACK RECORD

When shopping for an advisor, you can research his or her record. There are a couple of sources that you can use. You can check out advisors on the Securities and Exchange Commission (SEC) website or the Financial Industry Regulatory Authority (FINRA) website, depending on which license is held.

You would check out fiduciaries on the SEC website.

The letters after people's names indicate they have taken it upon themselves to get educated, pass a test, and pay a due or a fee to hold that credential. It doesn't necessarily mean that they're smarter. It just means that they were able to pass the test. However, the credential shows their willingness to take the time to grow and educate themselves.

What you really want to ask an advisor is "What do you do to keep yourself educated?" I can attest that I've spent probably 10 times the amount of money on my professional development that I spent on getting both a bachelor's and a master's degree.

My schooling didn't stop when I walked with my cap and gown. I attend professional conferences and am part of mentoring groups, including the Ed Slott Elite IRA Advisory Group. I take time out of my life. I must pass two tests a year. Not only does that studying assure my competence, but it also gives me access to a host of other up-to-date people.

If your advisor is not keeping current, how can he or she offer you the best advice? It would seem that such advisors are really just positioning a particular product. They know about that product, but as time passes, they need to keep learning. Other professionals have to go through certification—attorneys, for example, and pilots. Education is crucial. The letters after the name show one thing, but the extent of continuing education and professional development speaks volumes more.

FORBIDDEN REFERENCES

We're not allowed in our industry to provide references, a regulation with which I wholly disagree. The SEC will not allow fiduciaries to use current clients as references. People have asked for references, and I would love to comply, but I cannot. The regulation is onerous and, I believe, harmful to the industry.

THE GUT FEELING

Never underestimate your intuition. How do you feel when you look the advisor in the eye as you chat? Do you like him or her? Are you wondering whether this could ever work? In his book *Blink*, Malcolm Caldwell points out that first impressions—those gut feelings we get—are remarkably accurate.

Just because an advisor has plenty of credentials doesn't suggest a special concoction or way of doing anything. In the world of finances and financial advising, we all have access to similar tools. What's important is how they are applied and the knowledge brought to the fore in doing so. Good advisors, no matter what designations follow their name, will search for the best solutions using the latest tools and the latest rules for using them.

Learn all you can about the advisor's background and take note of the education and the credentials, but keep them in context. There are plenty of highly educated academics out there who can't seem to get along with people. You want someone who is not only qualified but also personable and eager to help you.

CHAPTER FOUR

Things That Go Bump

An old Scottish prayer goes like this: "From ghoulies and ghosties, and long-leggedy beasties, and things that go bump in the night, good Lord deliver us!" You probably don't believe in ghosts, but you can be certain that there are some beasties out there that can threaten your financial well-being. Retirees, in particular, need to be wary of a variety of risks that can wreck their dreams for the future.

Risk management is a major part of what I do, and it's a key function of a good financial advisor. It's the reason for our four-step review, which pays particular attention to the range of risks that retirees face.

Most people think of risk as just the prospect of losing money in the market. There are a variety of others.

Retirees face inflation risk. They face the risk of higher taxes, or unexpected ones. They could become seriously ill and need long-term care. They may simply live longer than their money can support them. And there are others: The hidden fees in some investments can drain away a significant amount of one's return. For retirees who have kept their investments in bonds, they face the risk that the interest rate will rise and harm that market.

Let's take a closer look at some of those pitfalls, starting with a major one and the one that most people associate with risk:

MARKET RISK

Unless you invest wisely and responsibly, a millionaire nest egg can be depleted to a fraction of what it was. We know the markets will move up and down. That's just what they do. And if you are invested heavily in a market that is falling, and if, at the same time, you need that money for living expenses, you and your portfolio are in trouble. Your retirement plan hinges on how well you manage market risk.

If you retired at the beginning of 1982, you saw the market go up a tremendous amount while you were still drawing money. If you retired in 2000, you suffered two of the biggest downturns since the Great Depression at the same time you began drawing income from your nest egg. When a downturn in the market slams you right as you're retiring, and in the immediate years after retirement, you have a big problem. When you have many up years before encountering a downturn, you fare far better. This is known as sequence of return risk.

SEQUENCE OF RETURN RISK EXAMPLE:

ARCHIE				EDITH			
Age	Hypothetical Market gains or losses	Withdrawl at start of year	Nest Egg at start of year	Age	Hypothetical Market gains or losses	Withdrawl at start of year	Nest Egg at start of year
64			$500,000	64			$500,000
65	-10.14%	$25,000	$500,000	65	12.78%	$25,000	$500,000
66	-13.04%	$25,750	$426,839	66	23.45%	$25,750	$535,716
67	-23.37%	$26,523	$348,776	67	26.38%	$26,523	$629,575
68	14.62%	$27,318	$246,956	68	3.53%	$27,318	$762,140
69	2.03%	$28,138	$251,750	69	13.62%	$28,138	$760,755
70	12.40%	$28,982	$228,146	70	3.00%	$26,982	$832,396
71	27.25%	$29,851	$223,862	71	-38.49%	$29,851	$827,524
72	-6.56%	$30,747	$246,879	72	26.38%	$30,747	$490,684
73	26.31%	$31,669	$201,956	73	19.53%	$31,669	$581,270
74	4.46%	$32,619	$215,084	74	26.67%	$32,619	$656,916
75	7.06%	$33,598	$190,610	75	31.01%	$33,598	$790,788
76	-1.54%	$34,606	$168,090	76	20.26%	$34,606	$991,981
77	34.11%	$35,644	$131,429	77	34.11%	$35,644	$1,151,375
78	20.26%	$36,713	$128,458	78	-1.54%	$36,713	$1,496,314
79	31.01%	$37,815	$110,335	79	7.00%	$37,815	$1,437,133
80	26.67%	$38,949	$95,008	80	4.46%	$38,949	$1,498,042
81	19.53%	$40,118	$71,009	81	26.31%	$40,118	$1,524,231
82	26.38%	$36,923	$36,923	82	-6.56%	$41,321	$1,874,535
83	-38.49%	$0	$0	83	27.25%	$42,561	$1,712,970
84	3.00%			84	12.40%	$43,638	$2,125,604
85	13.62%			85	2.03%	$45,153	$2,339,923
86	3.53%			86	14.62%	$46,507	$2,341,297
87	26.38%			87	-23.37%	$47,903	$2,630,297
88	23.45%			88	-13.04%	$49,340	$1,978,993
89	12.78%			89	-10.14%	$50,820	$1,677,975
Average return			Total withdrawl	Average return			Total withdrawl
8.03%			$580,963	8.03%			$911,482

Let's say two people retire, Archie and Edith, and each has a nest egg of $500,000. Over the next 25 years, the rate of return for each retiree averages 8.03 percent. Each heads into retirement after age 64 with that same amount.

Although the returns average the same, imagine that they got them in the exact opposite order. Archie had negative years at the beginning of his retirement, and the positive years didn't come until later. Edith had positive years starting out, with the negative years later on. Their returns, in other words, mirrored each other.

Each withdrew money, starting at 5 percent and increasing each year for inflation. Archie was out of money by age 83. Edith's account grew and, at age 89, her nest egg was $1.6 million. And that's an immense difference, even though both could say they averaged 8.03 percent in retirement. That's a graphic example of sequence of return risk. So much depends on when you start taking money out. We don't know when the years of bad markets will occur.

Wall Street wants you to take that risk. The stockbrokers who want you to invest your portfolio in equities are fine either way. They make money whether you do well or not. As we have seen, it's usually all about the transactions in that world. They don't want you to leave the world of risk.

Think of it this way: You have a sports car and think it's time to get more conservative and buy something with four-wheel drive, such as an SUV. You go to your favorite dealership and tell the salesman what you want, and he shows you a new sports car. You ask to see something more conservative, and he shows you a sports car of a different color. You get frustrated and walk out, but you turn back and see the sign over the dealership, marked with the words "Sports Cars." You realize that the salesman was trying to sell you the best stuff he had, which was sports cars. He did not have four-wheel drive cars or SUVs on the lot.

That's what it is like working with a Wall Street-type firm. It only has risk-based solutions for your plan. It's very true that as you take greater risks, the potential for a greater return is there. Wall Street will compare its performance to the S&P. If you're looking at active management, they're always going to say, "How did we do relative to the S&P?" If the market goes down by 25 percent, they actually consider it a win if you only lost 22 percent.

You never see a sports team that's happy after losing, even if it was a close game. Has anyone ever poured champagne at the end of the World Series because the team only lost by one run? That one point is the difference between win and lose, between glee and gloom.

So it makes little sense to just look at how your account moves relative to an unmanaged index. Instead, you want to know whether your assets are in keeping with a plan that you have in place. Don't congratulate yourself if you're just not as big a loser as some other people out there. You don't want to be a loser at all.

I got a call, once, from a client who asked why his portfolio had not done as well as the market. He had done well. At that time, his return was about 9 percent.

"But why am I not doing as well as the market?" he asked. I had to tell him his investment was not designed to beat the market. What it was designed to do was implement his plan.

"In the plan that we worked out together," I explained, "we assumed we only needed to get 5 percent for your plan to be successful and for you to have the retirement that you were looking for. Why take on additional risk if you don't have to?"

The stockbrokers' perspective, by contrast, is to wait out the storm. "Just buy and hold," they say, "and you will be all right." Buy and hold is fine for some markets. For other markets, it's going to do you in. A little simple math will show you how hard it is to get back to even once you take a hard punch.

Then, there's the opportunity cost of what your money could have been accomplishing, how it could have grown, had it not been depleted so soon. Let's say you have $100,000 and lose 30 percent, which cuts your account down to $70,000. If, instead, you had kept the money in a safe account earning 3 percent, you would have $103,000. You would be better off by $33,000. It would mean that the $70,000 would have to earn 43 percent just to get back to $100,000 and break even. To catch up with the $103,000, it would need to gain 47.14 percent in one year. Those are pretty big returns to chase, and would you likely be putting your money to such risk after losing 30 percent in a year?

It gets even worse if you're taking income from the tumbling account. Let's say that you also need a 4 percent income from that $100,000. That would leave you with $66,000. That would mean your gain to break even would have to be 51.5 percent in the first year. To catch up with the $103,000 that you could have realized if you had invested the money in a safe account, you would need a return of 56 percent.

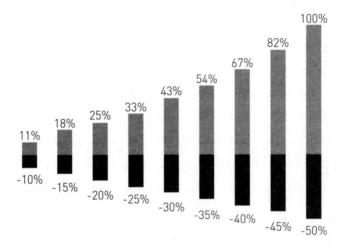

This chart represents how much return it takes to overcome a loss. It will always take more return because you're working with less money after a loss.

"I am more concerned about the return *of* my money than the return *on* my money," Mark Twain said. His wry observation is quite apt for those transitioning from their accumulation years to preservation and distribution. The implications for a retiree's dreams and lifestyle are huge.

A WORD TO BOND INVESTORS

Let's turn our attention to the bond market, where another risk threatens countless retirees. It's the prospect of rising interest rates, and with rates so low, they are likely to go up.

Many people keep their retirement plan and other portfolios in a balance of stocks and bonds. They subscribe to the traditional thinking that bonds counteract stocks, providing a safety net if the stock market crashes. The common advice is to transition to a higher ratio of bonds to stocks as one gets older. That is put forward as more conservative and safer.

Both stocks and bonds, however, are in the world of risk. No matter what investments Wall Street puts you into, they just have a different flavor of risk. So, by transitioning from stocks to bonds, you're trading in market risk for interest rate risk.

For the last 30 years, bonds have indeed proven to be safe. But there is an inverse relationship between interest rates and bond prices. As rates fall, the prices rise, and vice versa. As we know, interest rates have been falling for an extended time.

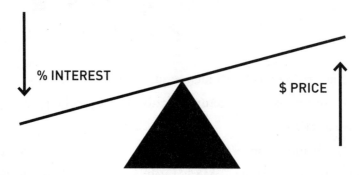

Those prices are based on the ten-year Treasury note. In 1981 a ten-year note paid 15.84 percent interest. That meant a $100,000 investment would bring in an annual check for $15,840. Not bad. Those were high-interest days, albeit high inflation days too.

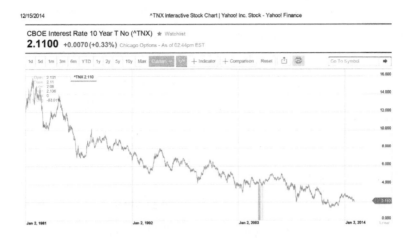

Source: Yahoo Finance

The interest rates have since decreased over 80 percent. That's been good for bond prices. In today's environment, consequently, bond values have gone up. The bond that you bought at 15.84 percent is more attractive in comparison to the newer prevailing rate.

As I write this, the Federal Reserve continues a policy of keeping interest rates as low as possible. When it stops doing that and rates rise, bond values will tumble. That means that bond holders today face a significant risk.

You may hear the sound of a bubble bursting. Bonds have been good for many years, but they are firmly in the world of risk. Trouble likely lies ahead.

Investors sometimes have been advised to revisit their portfolios and rebalance their stock and bond mix as they get older, leaning more heavily toward bonds. Clearly, you would do so at your peril. Such rebalancing does not reduce risk; it merely trades risk.

Instead, you should shift into an alternative so that your investments truly become safer the older you get. Traditionally, when you rebalance, you take your winning stocks or winning positions, sell some of them, and buy your losing positions at a discount. But you can choose to rebalance your portfolio in a way that truly distributes your investments between the worlds of safety and risk in a manner consistent with your income needs in retirement.

INFLATION RISK

Inflation poses another major risk to your life's savings. Here's a way to put inflation in perspective. Ask yourself how much you paid for your first house. Then, ask yourself how much you paid for your most recent car. Especially if you are in your mid-to-late sixties or seventies, it is likely that you paid less for your first house than your most recent car. That illustrates dramatically how prices have risen.

While you're working, inflation doesn't affect you as much if you get raises at work. Your income increases as you are promoted or change jobs. Once you go to a fixed income, you soon see how inflation affects you a lot more. You need to have a plan for combating inflation, which means your income must increase to keep pace with inflation.

Certain costs that are particularly important for the elderly are also particularly vulnerable to inflation. Medical costs have increased at a pace faster than the overall inflation rate. As they increase, they hit the elderly hardest of all at a time when they most need medical services. In Chapter 8, we'll take a closer look at health-care and long-term-care issues.

You may recall the heyday of CDs, when rates were well into the double digits, in the late 1970s and early 1980s. But those rates must be viewed from the perspective of inflation. In 1979 the CPI increased 11.3 percent. In 1980 it was 13.5 percent. In 1981 it was 10.3 percent. And so, as attractive as those CD rates might have seemed, they never really kept pace with inflation. Both were experiencing double-digit times. To think that CDs were a good hedge was simply wrong.

What, then, is a good hedge against inflation these days? A retiree might come to the conclusion that there is little choice but to accept market risk. That's the traditional thinking. Traditionally, stocks have been a better hedge against inflation than other types of fixed securities or fixed income, CDs, bonds, and the like.

What people often have yet to learn about are alternatives that could get them a high level of safety. They could get the same safety that a CD has but also the opportunity to beat inflation or at least keep up with it. Most people haven't been exposed to what else is available out there other than the usual lineup of stocks and mutual funds and bonds and CDs.

You can prepare for inflation, but there is nothing you can do about it. Inflation will happen. It's out of your control. So you want to look to some other risks, ones that you can control.

OTHER RISKS

One of those is the risk that taxation poses to your portfolio, and another is the risk of investment fees that can eat away at the value of your return. Those are important elements when we do a four-step review of a client's financial situation. One of the first steps in our four-step review is a tax analysis to find any money that is falling through the cracks. You can influence the amount of the tax bite through careful planning.

The fundamental questions are these: How can you eliminate unnecessary taxation on your investments, which can boost your return? How can you reduce some of the risk in your portfolio or your investments so that you don't have that affecting you as well?

Besides taxes, you also face the drain of the hidden fees in mutual funds and other places where they erode your return. You may not even be aware of those fees. I'll explain more on tax issues in the next chapter and on investment fees in Chapter 6.

THE BIGGEST RISK OF ALL

All of those risks really play into one central risk: the risk of longevity, or simply, the possibility of outliving one's money. Once, people knew it was very likely that they were only going to make it into their midsixties, which was the typical lifespan not so long ago. When Social Security was instituted, for example, no one expected people to live as long as they do today.

If you knew you weren't going to live all that long, many of the issues of retirement planning you are reading about in this book would not be so important. They would all be moot if we were to die sooner. But we are living longer and longer, creating greater urgency for effective planning.

CHAPTER FIVE

Tax Attacks

Tina and Jerry Clark were doing well in life. Jerry was a high-level executive with many years at the same company. He had a great salary with generous stock options. The couple had been careful to save, spending less than they made and investing the rest for their future.

They participated in their 401(k), making contributions to the maximum. They weren't able to tuck money away into a Roth IRA because they made too much, but they plowed money into a variety of other accounts and investments. They believed they were doing all the right things.

They were not.

They found out what was happening when they came in for a four-step evaluation. Those accounts in which they were squirreling their investments were fully taxable. I showed them on their tax return how much they had paid in unnecessary income taxes: $32,000.

They were totally unaware of that. In fact, they were flabbergasted. That amounted to a couple of nice vacations and maybe a new car. Instead, they gave it to Uncle Sam.

What happened? In short, they were paying tax on money that they were not spending. They were automatically reinvesting taxable dividends, for example, and the carrying costs for all those positions were far more than pocket change.

It's a fundamental of good tax planning that if you have money you do not intend to spend soon, you need to find investments that will not result in a tax on the earnings. There are tax-efficient ways to accumulate money for your retirement.

You may be wondering, as the Clarks did, whether you are making that mistake. How do you know if you are paying tax on money you are not spending? The answer is on your tax return. Look at the taxable income listed on lines 8, 9, and 13 of tax form 1040. If you see income on those lines and it isn't money you are spending, you are paying tax unnecessarily. Line 8 is interest. Line 9 is dividends. Line 13 is capital gains. If you don't need that money for living expenses, you should find ways not to pay tax on it. You may be handing over a fortune to the government unnecessarily.

Imagine this scenario: Your teenage son finally joins you for breakfast after taking a long shower, but he has left the water running. "Why, on God's green earth, is the shower still running?" you ask. "Well, I have the temperature set just right, so it will be perfect when I take another shower after school," he explains. How would you react?

That's how it appears to us when we see people growing their investments to generate taxable income that isn't going toward living expenses. People who hold money in taxable accounts, whether brokerage accounts or mutual funds, need to think that through carefully. Every year, good money is draining away to taxes. You need to turn off the faucet when you aren't in the shower.

Poor tax planning doesn't necessarily result in some major, sudden blow. For most people, the money leaks through the cracks, year after year after year, but it diminishes a nest egg nonetheless. Once you have ceded that money to the government, you lose the opportunity to ever make any interest or returns on it. It's never coming back to you.

Your goal should be to maintain control of your money as much as possible. If the government is going to get its take eventually, then at least postpone it as long as you can, because, in the meantime, you can leverage it to your advantage.

You can be sure that the government has its eye on all the untaxed money that people have been putting into retirement plans for decades. Those assets today amount to $20 trillion, and the government wants its share. Taxes are the government's only way of raising revenue, and it needs revenue more than ever. Today's retirees are a prime source. Uncle Sam finally gets his tax every time that money is withdrawn from those accounts and whenever it is left to somebody else.

It's not hard to see why a tax analysis is the very first part of our four-step review. That highlights how significant this risk is. It's one of the first things that I need to talk about with new clients. We need to stop the bleeding wherever possible.

TAXABLE, TAX DEFERRED, TAX-FREE

When it comes to taxes, money comes in three flavors: taxable, tax deferred, and tax-free.

Taxable money is the income on which you currently pay tax. If you look at your 1040 form, again going down those lines, it's wages, interest, dividends, capital gains, rental real estate, pensions, farm income, distributions from retirement plans, and up to 85 percent of your Social Security benefit.

THE THREE TAX BUCKETS

TAXABLE	TAX-DEFERRED	TAX-FREE

GOAL →

TAXABLE	TAX-DEFERRED	TAX-FREE
• Wages	• Qualified Plans	• Roth IRAs
• Interest	• Savings Bonds	• Municipal Bonds (Interest)
• Dividends	• Annuities	• Life Insurance
• Capital Gains		
• Rental Income		
• Pension		
• Social Security (up to 85%)		
• Qualified Plan Distributions		

The next category is tax-deferred money. That's money on which you won't need to pay tax until you withdraw it for use. The money within those retirement plans is tax deferred from the time it is invested until the money is withdrawn, and the government, of course, eventually insists that it be withdrawn. Savings bonds are tax deferred. I used to get those from my grandmother at Christmas time. They were a fun gift. Capital assets, such as land or company stock, are tax deferred until you sell them. The growth is deferred until you sell the asset. You don't pay tax on it every year, but it'll go back to being taxable as capital gains when you do sell. Annuities are tax-deferred investments as well.

The next category is even better: tax-free. There are only three things that are tax-free: Roth IRAs, the interest earned on municipal bonds, and life insurance.

If you had your choice, in which of those three categories would you rather have more money? As you turn the pages of this book, you will see the significance of these categories and their significance in effective income and estate planning. It's important to correlate these categories to the various purposes you intend for your money.

TAX DRAG ON YOUR RETURN

If we look over the last 20 years, the S&P 500 unmanaged index has returned 9.22 percent. It incurs no taxation, no fees, and no expense. It's just the pure index, in all of its glory.

However, the return for the average equity investor over the last 20 years has been 5.02 percent, according to a DALBAR study that tracks investor returns and behavior.

So why is there such a disparity between the unmanaged index and the average investor's return? Fees and taxation are two of the biggest reasons. Taxation could actually cause investors to miss out on doubling their money. People don't make the connection to how much tax they are paying, and the reason is that they don't pay it out of the pocket where their investments are. They pay the tax via some other source.

They never go back and look at their return and subtract the tax they paid on that investment. They never make that connection. Their broker will never tell them that, because at the bottom of every brokerage statement, if you look closely enough, you will find words to this effect: "Consult your tax advisor. We are not tax advisors."

PHANTOM INCOME TAX

Phantom income taxation is paying tax on something that doesn't exist. Let's suppose that at the beginning of the year, you have $100,000 in a mutual fund that is in a taxable account.

Now, throughout the year, that mutual fund is actively managed. The fund will buy and sell securities and receive dividends. And it doesn't pay tax. It has to send that to the shareholders of the fund. Even though you never received a dime from the fund because you have everything reinvested into the fund, the government looks at it as if the fund sent you a check. It's still a transaction in the eyes of the government, so it's taxable, even though you endorsed it back to the fund to buy more shares.

Let's say on a cold day in February you go to your mailbox and find a form from your mutual fund company called a 1099. You open it up and learn that the mutual fund throughout the year generated $10,000 in dividends and capital gains.

Now, what if this was a year when the markets were unfavorable, and at the end of this year, your account value was roughly $80,000? This means you lost $20,000 of what you had at the beginning of the year. But you still have this $10,000 distribution.

Can a mutual fund still pay out dividends and capital gains and lose money? Absolutely it can. So, you go to your tax preparer. He says he has great news. Because of your tax bracket, your dividends and capital gains are only taxed at 15 percent, not 20 percent, as they used to be. Nonetheless, you paid $1,500 in tax for the privilege of losing $20,000 of your wealth. That's phantom income tax.

That can certainly catch people by surprise. It can seem so fundamentally unfair, yet it's the way the system works. In 2008 the market decreased by 37 percent. The mutual fund industry paid out billions in dividends and capital gains that year, even though the investors lost money.

This is why mutual funds are extremely tax-inefficient vehicles. They're taxed three ways. They're taxed on dividends; they're taxed on the capital gains when securities are sold; and they're taxed on the appreciation of the shares, which is why mutual funds should be held in a more tax-efficient account, such as a 401(k), an IRA, or a Roth.

THE TRUTH ABOUT RETIREMENT PLANS

When tax-deferred retirement plans—the 401(k)s and the IRAs and similar vehicles that are ubiquitous today—appeared in the late 1970s and early '80s, they were heralded as a great deal that would take care of the investor in retirement. People jumped at the opportunity to get a break from the IRS. The reasoning was that the tax wouldn't be due until the money was withdrawn during retirement, and they would be in a lower tax bracket then. In the meantime, their accounts could grow without a tax hit.

Be advised: there's something more to consider.

Imagine you are starting a business, and you have a partner who draws up plans for how it will operate. He decides how much money can go into it and determines all the nuances, all the rules and regulations by which you will abide.

You agree and put all your money into the business. In good faith, you work hard, trying to do the things to help the business grow. Meanwhile, your partner sits in a back room playing solitaire. And some of his actions do not exactly help the cause. He makes decisions that cut into the profits.

Thirty-five years later, you have grown the company to a significant size. Nearing retirement, you are ready to start reaping the benefits so you have the income to support the lifestyle you dreamed about. You are ready to sell the company.

Out of the back room comes your partner, holding out his palm, and it's not for a handshake. He wants his cut. He wants a share of every distribution you take out of the business. And you don't get to tell him how much he will get. He tells you.

Your partner has a long, white beard and wears a star-spangled top hat. You are looking into the stern countenance of Uncle Sam. Most savvy businesspeople would not let a partner treat them that way, but that, in essence, is what is happening to the myriads of 401(k) investors.

Consider your 401(k) to be like an animal pen. Farmers entice animals into their pens by laying out some food for them, something to attract them. The IRS and Wall Street have set up this pen called a 401(k). In there, they've put three troughs of food to lure you in. One trough is the tax deductibility of whatever money you put into the plan. That's a nice feature. They put in tax deferral, which means you're not going to pay tax on any of the growth while you're in the pen. That's a great feature.

You may also have employer match, which is free money, yet another great feature. You frolic right on into the pen, and the door behind you slams shut. And you start to fatten up.

Now, how do you get out of the pen? You have to go through IRS processing. The agency will take a few pounds of flesh off you as you get out.

Think of the trillions of dollars that are in these retirement plans. The government is eyeing that. Uncle Sam can manipulate the tax code to tell you how much he will get from the plans.

Do you believe you will be in a lower tax bracket when you retire? You may be in a higher tax bracket. You don't know what's going to happen with the brackets. And don't we all aspire to make more money in the years ahead, not less?

You're indeed avoiding taxation along the way, the theory being that you will be in a lower tax bracket in retirement, but you could be deferring yourself into quite a mess. It could be quite the opposite of what you expected. You could be in a higher tax bracket, and the tax rate itself could be higher.

We're at a historically low tax rate, and taxes are, effectively, going to rise. It's almost inevitably going to happen. The rates are bound to get closer to the historical average. During World War II and into the 1950s, the top bracket approached and exceeded 90 percent. It was 70 percent in the 1970s. Today's rate is much lower—it was 39.6 percent for 2014—but considering our national debt and political pressures, the direction it will take seems clear.

INCOME TAXES

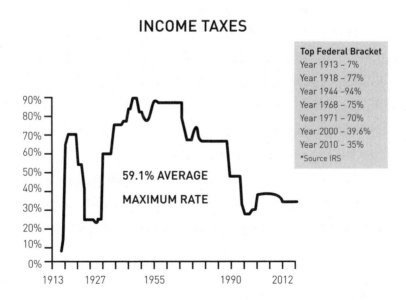

Top Federal Bracket
Year 1913 – 7%
Year 1918 – 77%
Year 1944 –94%
Year 1968 – 75%
Year 1971 – 70%
Year 2000 – 39.6%
Year 2010 – 35%
*Source IRS

59.1% AVERAGE

MAXIMUM RATE

THE GOLDEN DECADE

The first several years of retirement are what we call the golden decade. They are critical years in which you have the most control over your tax situation.

At age 70 you reach two trigger points. One, your Social Security benefit will no longer grow. Until you are 70, you can postpone your benefit, and the amount you eventually get will be greater. But that increase stops at age 70. You are not forced to take the benefit, but you have reached the maximum.

Second, when you are age 70½ you have to start venturing out of the pen. Your tax-deferment days are coming to an end. You have to take annual required minimum distributions (RMDs) from your retirement plan, and the amount you must withdraw increases every year. Uncle Sam wants his taxes from you. And if you don't pony up, he will assess you a penalty of 50 percent of what you were supposed to pull out.

However, in that golden decade, from age 60 to 70, you have a time frame in which you can control your own destiny. You can do strategic rollouts of your IRAs to convert them into Roth IRAs. More retirees are entering retirement without a pension now. This is where you have control. You can do this advanced planning to limit the IRS's impact on your retirement plans.

At 70½, once you get your RMDs, you cannot use those payouts to roll into a Roth. That's prohibited. You certainly can still contribute to a Roth IRA after that age, but in order to do so, you need earned income.

A CONTINUING TREND

Despite all these considerations, deferred-tax retirement plans have become the primary means by which most people today are saving for retirement, and that, of course, is no small matter. They are counting on that money to last the rest of their lives. For many people, these plans are indeed a good deal, particularly if the employer provides a matching amount for the employee's contribution. That's free money. And tax deferral has the great benefit of allowing you to leverage money for growth that otherwise would go to the government up front. As we have seen, that is a valuable element in financial planning.

What's important is to understand the path that you are on when you invest in these retirement plans. You are creating tax ramifications down the road. It comes down to getting the money out in the most tax efficient way possible.

In the adult education classes that I teach, I point out how the emphasis on retirement planning has switched from traditional pensions (defined benefit) to the deferred-tax contribution plans (defined contribution). In 1992, defined benefit plans still covered 32 percent of the people. In 2012 that was down to 17 percent. Meanwhile, in that same period, defined contribution coverage went from 35 percent to 41 percent.

That trend is continuing as more and more Americans enter retirement with large 401(k) balances that are meant to provide them with retirement income for a lifetime.

HOW TO "STRETCH" YOUR IRA

The tax implications extend beyond the lifetime of the IRA holder. If you do not use up all the money during your lifetime, your heirs can face a major tax consequence when the money is left to them in a lump sum. A lump sum payment forces the recipient into a high tax bracket, thereby forfeiting a significant amount of the money in taxes.

You can do something about that. IRS guidelines provide for what is known as a "stretch," meaning that the individual who inherits the money does not necessarily have to accept it as a lump sum. The stretch provision allows the heir to receive annual distributions, based on life expectancy. In other words, some of the tax deferment is stretched out for the lifetime of the recipients.

As for 401(k)s and other types of qualified plans, whether you can set up a stretch depends on what the particular plan will allow. Most lack the infrastructure to support the stretch and do not want the record-keeping expense.

The stretch provision is permissible under current tax law, but there has been talk of limiting it to spouses. It's another example of Uncle Sam wanting his money right away and closing the doors to further delays. But for now, the stretch is a highly attractive provision. The amount of money that is not withdrawn continues to grow in the heir's account without being taxed.

Let's say a 65-year-old couple has a $100,000 IRA, and it's not an account that they really need. Let's assume they can earn a 6 percent rate of return on it, and they take out only what is required by the IRS (RMD) and leave whatever's left to their daughter. If the daughter, in turn, only takes out what's required, based on her life expectancy, she'll receive $598,000 in withdrawals from the account over her lifetime. So, a $100,000 account can turn into a $640,000 family legacy.

If current tax law stands, when the daughter passes away, she can also leave that money as a stretch provision to her own heirs, say, her children and grandchildren. This could become multigenerational wealth, all starting from a fairly modest IRA.

But it could only become such a family fortune if it's handled properly and the recipients resist temptations over the course of those generations. You cannot simply require that your heirs take the money as a stretch. It's a choice that your heirs get to make. After you are gone, they will check a box and receive the money either as a lump sum or as a stretch.

You have to do some restrictive estate planning if you want to force your beneficiaries to do the stretch. There are ways that you can do that through the use of various trust documents. An attorney or a trust department will manage that arrangement and will take a fee from the money that otherwise would have gone to the heirs.

Short of setting up a trust, the best way to help your heirs avoid the tax consequences of a lump sum distribution is to have a family meeting and explain the benefits of using the stretch and to make your intentions clear to all. That way, you educate them up front about what you want them to do.

You might say something like this: "Look, this is tax-toxic money. If you take it out in a lump sum, it's going to be as if you earned the same amount of money at some job, and you are going to go into the higher tax brackets and give a lot of it back to the IRS. That's not my intention. What I want you to do is use the tax laws to your advantage and only take out what the government requires you to take out. Here's an idea: Why don't you use that amount to do doing something fun once a year, maybe a trip with the kids, and consider it to be on Mom and Dad. Do something to remember us by. Don't give most of it to the IRS."

The lure of the lump sum is hard to resist, particularly for a young person who lacks much experience in dealing with finances. That's why a family meeting can help so much. If your desires go unspoken, how will they be heard?

IS A ROTH FOR YOU?

A Roth IRA differs from a traditional IRA in that you pay no income tax on the distributions from it. However, you do not get a tax deduction up front for any contributions that you put into a Roth, as you do with a traditional IRA. The government gets its tax money right away rather than down the road. The trade-off is that the investor eventually withdraws the money tax-free.

A Roth IRA will operate under the same parameters as a traditional IRA, with a couple of exceptions. With a Roth, you have to keep the money in the account for five years from when you make your first contribution. If you take money out sooner, you are assessed a penalty. After five years, you can take your contributions out without penalty, but you cannot take out your earnings without penalty until you are age 59½. There are provisions to get earnings out earlier for medical expenses, first-time home purchase, education, and for paying your taxes. The government sees fit to skip the penalty if it means it gets its money.

How do you know whether a Roth IRA or a traditional IRA is the best choice for you? The question to ask yourself is whether you think the tax rate will be higher when you reach retirement than it is now. If you believe that will be the case, you definitely should consider the Roth. If you can do both, do both. A rule of thumb has been that if you have a qualified plan at work, and you have employer matching, you should contribute as much as you must to get 100 percent of that free money. Then, put the rest of the money you are setting aside for savings into a Roth IRA. That way, you're building tax-free retirement income.

CONVERTING TO A ROTH

Imagine you are a farmer getting ready to plant your crops. The IRS agent stops by and tells you that you can either pay the tax now on the seed that you're about to put in the ground, or he will come back in the fall and collect tax on the harvest. Neither of you know what that tax will be at harvest time. You both know what the tax is now. And you might want to pay up front because the tax, later in the year, just might be quite a bit higher.

Everyone assumes taxes are going up. Everyone loves the idea of having tax-free income. Everyone loves the idea of the Roth IRA and asks about converting a traditional plan into a Roth. But when we go through the analysis of how much tax it costs to convert, our clients are less excited.

You will want to consider your current tax bracket and what you think it will be in the future. What rate of return will you earn on the money, and how long do you think you will live? Those are the four factors to consider when determining whether a Roth conversion is right for you. The longer you live, the more you can make on the money, and the better the Roth conversion is going to be.

It's not an all-or-nothing choice. You don't have to convert 100 percent of your IRA to a Roth IRA. You can convert pieces of it. I call it a strategic rollout, or converting a portion of your IRA every year to manage your current tax bracket. If you are $20,000 away from entering the 28 percent bracket and you're still in the 25 percent bracket, take the $20,000 out. Keep it in the 25 percent bracket. Next year, do a conversion again.

There is no limit on how often you can do conversions. You can do a conversion before you're 59½. You can convert any time. The IRS removed the rules for age and income, so anyone of any income level can convert, and anyone at any age can convert. So, it's not considered a withdrawal from your IRA to convert into a Roth IRA. You won't get hit with the penalty. You just pay the tax on the converted amount. It is much like flipping a switch, and your account goes from being an IRA to a Roth IRA. There's a distribution code on the 1099 form that will indicate it was converted.

The unique thing about the Roth IRA is it's one of the few accounts that you can do over. When I was a kid playing kickball, I loved do-overs. If someone didn't roll the ball right, you could insist on their doing it over. Life has far too few do-overs. But you get one with a Roth conversion. If you do this conversion and are later shocked at your tax bill, you can go back and unwind the transaction.

Maybe the tax is just too much for you to bear. Maybe the account has since lost value and you don't want to pay tax on money that doesn't exist. You don't need a reason. I remember watching Seinfeld tell a clerk he was returning something "just for spite." It wasn't a good enough reason for that, but if that's why you want a redo on your Roth conversion, no problem. You can re-characterize it back to an IRA, and then, after a waiting period, you can convert it again under more favorable circumstances.

HOW TO GET A ROTH IF YOU MAKE TOO MUCH

Over a certain level of income, you cannot contribute to a Roth IRA, according to government regulations. That level changes each year. As I write this, it's $188,000 for a married couple. If you're single and you make over $127,000, you cannot contribute to a Roth IRA. So, if you're making over that amount, the government does not allow you the same benefit. It's like paying twice as much as the passenger next to you for a seat on an airplane. This doesn't seem fair.

But that does not prevent you from converting to a Roth IRA.

The current contribution limit is $5,500 if you are under age 50, or $6,500 if you are over age 50. If you are willing to put that amount of money into an account that brings you no tax deduction, you are willing to spend it anyway. So why not use it to pay the tax to convert some of your existing IRA? In a 25 percent tax bracket, $6,500 would convert $26,000 of an IRA to a Roth IRA. The larger converted amount will have a bigger impact on your retirement nest egg.

A lot of people in high-income brackets think the Roth is out of reach for them because the IRS says they can't contribute, but it doesn't prevent converting. That means they can take the same amount of money that they would like to contribute and use it to do a conversion.

A GOOD USE FOR YOUR RMD

Think about each year when you take out the RMD from your retirement account. How will you use that RMD? Will you spend it or reinvest it? If all you are taking out is the minimum, you probably don't need it for living expenses or you would be withdrawing considerably more than what the government demands.

If you earn interest, dividends, or capital gains, you will pay taxes, and, again, since all you are taking out is the RMD, you will be paying those taxes on resources you probably don't even need. In that case, the better alternative is to leverage the withdrawal into a tax-free asset.

How do you do that? Consider what the tax code provides. Municipal bond interest is tax exempt, but as far as concerns accounts that are tax-free, there are only two: the Roth IRA, and life insurance. As I pointed out, you can't put the withdrawal into a Roth. That leaves life insurance as a strategy that can effectively help you to disinherit the IRS from your IRA.

As you begin to convert your IRA into life insurance, you will be doing your heirs a big favor. Instead of getting a taxable lump sum from your retirement account, they will be getting a tax-free payout from your policy.

YOUR FAIR SHARE

Once, and only once, I heard a client actually say, "I don't mind paying taxes." All the others whom I have ever helped to find ways to save on taxes have been adamant about paying only what they legally must.

In the largest sense, paying taxes is how we all contribute to the social welfare, to the roads and the bridges and the infrastructure of our society, but the tax breaks that are in the code are there for a reason. Those tax breaks are meant to encourage certain behaviors that the government deems beneficial, and it is perfectly ethical to take advantage of them to the greatest extent possible.

The government, however, will not tell you how to find those breaks. The IRS will not contact you to say, "Hey, by the way, did you know you could have paid less if you'd only done this?" It's up to you to learn, either on your own or by consulting a competent advisor.

Some might scowl at the thought that Warren Buffet pays a lower tax rate than his secretary, but that is a result of the tax treatment of different assets. He doesn't make a wage, so he is not taxed at ordinary income rates. Most of his wealth comes from dividends and capital gains, which are taxed at a lower rate because the government wants to spur investment in businesses. If he were earning ordinary income, he would pay a substantially higher rate than his secretary, but he's smart enough to develop his wealth via the means available to him.

Taxation does tend to have a much greater impact on retirees, who are living on a fixed income. Most retirees had taxes withdrawn from each paycheck. The employer took out the requisite amount and sent it to the government. Once retired, they have to send in a quarterly estimated tax payment. That's a hard transition for a lot of people.

When the tax payments come out of your check automatically, you pay less attention to them. Imagine we all received our entire gross paycheck in cash at a window each week and then had to immediately walk down a hall and, at each of several other windows, pay out sums for federal tax, Social Security, Medicare tax, and state, local, and city taxes; at each stop, a troll demanded payment for passage. I think we'd have a revolt or, at least, people would be more proactive about lowering their taxes.

But that's how it can be for retirees, which is why tax planning is such a hot topic for them. People come to believe that once money is in their bank account, it belongs to them. To send it back out goes against what they have done for decades. They feel as if they suddenly have one more huge bill, although it's a bill that has been there all along.

It's up to you to become aware of the tax consequences of your investments. And it's up to you to make sure you get the breaks you deserve. But you need not go down that path alone.

There are many wrong turns, and an astute advisor can steer you the right way.

CHAPTER SIX

The Secret Life of Fees

One emphasis of the four-step review that we do for clients is an examination of the fees that are charged on investment accounts. That is one of the major risks that retirees face, and it can drain away a significant amount of their retirement portfolio.

For the majority of Americans, the primary saving vehicle is a mutual fund. Mutual funds are notorious for having lots of fees, the majority of which are undisclosed. Mutual funds have both disclosed and undisclosed fees, whether they are loaded funds or no-load funds.

A load is different from a fee. A load is what you pay to acquire the investment. The fees are what you pay while holding the investment.

The load is actually the sales charge. If you paid the commission to buy the fund, that's what the load is. All mutual funds have fees. That's the charge that's being deducted from your account to operate the fund. If you're not going to do the investing on your own, you're going to pay others to do it for you, and they deserve to be compensated. They are going to charge for their expertise.

Those fees, however, sap away a lot of your potential for gain. And those fees don't come out only when the account makes money; they also come out when the account loses money. Fees reduce your gains, and they magnify your losses.

DISCLOSED AND UNDISCLOSED FEES

This is a major concern because so many people depend on the mutual funds in their retirement plans. Of the people who come through our system, 99.9 percent have mutual funds as their primary means of saving. Mutual funds are prevalent in every investment vehicle, and they are the number-one vehicle in 401(k) s, which is where most people build their wealth.

The disclosed fees are the ones stated in the prospectus. Those are the charges to "keep the lights on." They are the source of money to pay employees, managers, the building, leases, phones, utilities, and so on. They are how the company keeps the doors open.

The undisclosed fees result from the fund's activities during the year. At the beginning of the year, the mutual fund managers do not know how much they are going to trade, because they don't know the direction the market will take. As the markets unfold and the managers decide to buy this or sell that, they pay commissions on each trade. You would think that they would buy on an institutional level, but they pay commissions every time they buy and sell securities.

The *Wall Street Journal* carried out a study and reported that the undisclosed fees are brokers' commissions on trades, the bid and ask spread of the security itself, the market's impact on the cost of the trades, and the cash drag.

The study found that the trading cost for the average US stock fund came to about 1.44 percent of the assets. Some funds had a higher cost, some lower. That's in addition to the reported or disclosed expenses. You think you're paying 1 percent or maybe 1.5 percent, as stated in the prospectus, but you find that 1.44

percent of trading costs are also involved. Now you're closer to 3 percent.

Other expenses can claim almost an additional 1 percent: the market impact cost, the bid/ask spread, and the cash drag. The bid/ask spread is the difference between the buying price and the selling price of a security. Every security, throughout the trading day, has two prices: what I'm willing to sell my security for and what I'm willing to pay for yours. That difference changes throughout the day. It's not set. It moves throughout the day, based on supply and demand.

Think about when you buy a car. There's a retail and a wholesale price: what the dealership will give you for your car, and the price at which you can sell it to somebody else. That's the easiest way to think about it. The disparity is not that large in the stock market, but there still is a disparity between the two. And that represents a drain on the return.

Cash drag has a bigger impact in bad years. Mutual funds are comprised of stocks, bonds, and cash, in their simplest form. Most people have open-ended mutual funds, which means that at the end of the day you can call your fund company to redeem your shares for cash. The manager needs enough cash in the fund to meet those redemptions. If his funds have enough—and most funds do—it's fine. If his funds don't, he has to sell securities in order to raise the cash for the redemptions. All mutual funds will carry a certain amount of cash, but cash earns no return. That's the drag. If you wonder why you don't get the same returns that an index suggests you should, consider that disparity. The index incurs no expenses, no cash drag, and no taxation. Your fund has all of those issues in it.

That's why, if we look at the Dalbar study, which tracks investors' returns over the last 20 years, when the S&P has averaged 9.22 percent, the average equity investor has averaged 5.02 percent. The disparity is attributed to these fees and taxation issues along the way.

	Investor Returns[1]					
	Equity Funds	Asset Allocation Funds	Fixed Income Funds	Inflation	S&P 500	Barclays Aggregate Bond Index
Since QAIB Inception	3.69	1.85	0.70	2.80	11.11	7.67
20 Year	5.02	2.53	0.71	2.37	9.22	5.74
10 Year	5.88	2.63	0.63	2.38	7.40	4.55
5 Year	15.21	7.70	2.29	2.08	17.94	4.44
3 Year	10.87	6.26	0.70	2.07	16.18	3.27
12 Months	25.54	13.57	-3.66	1.52	32.41	-2.02

Source: "Quantitative Analysis of Investor Behavior, 2014," DALBAR, Inc.

[1]Average equity investor, average bond investor and average asset allocation investor performance results are calculated using data supplied by the Investment Company Institute. Investor returns are represented by the change in total mutural fund assets after excluding sales, redemptions and exchanges. This method of calculation captures realized and unrealized captial gains, dividends, interest, trading costs, sales charges, fees, expenses and any other costs. After calculation investor returns in dollar terms, two percentages are calculated for the period examined: Total investor return rate and annualized investor return rate. Total return rate is determined by calculating the investor return dollars as a percentage of the net sales, redemptions and exchanges for each period.

PROSPECTUS PARALYSIS

You can find the disclosed fees in the prospectus for your fund. I've been teaching classes for years and have spoken to thousands of people. Every time I ask people whether they have read their mutual funds prospectus, maybe one or two hands go up. Those are people with very thick glasses and a lot of time to spare. Yes, you should read the prospectus, but it is not exactly a page-turner.

The prospectus will have all of the other information pertaining to the fund, such as how it will be invested, who is managing the fund, their track records, their tenures, and major holdings within the fund. By the time that prospectus is printed and distributed, that information could have already changed. For the most up-to-date information on holdings, you always want to check the company's website.

The prospectus will only show you the disclosed fees. It will not explain any of the undisclosed fees, because fund managers don't know how much they will amount to in any given year. The clue for you, as an investor, is to look at the fund's turnover. The higher the turnover, the greater the expense. The greater the expense, the less money for you. That's easy to see. Third-party sources such as Morningstar will report turnovers. Normally, you can see it at the end of the year. You can also call the fund company and ask what its turnover ratio was for the year.

Some regulations have sought to bring greater transparency to expenses. The US Department of Labor, which regulates 401(k)s, is looking at disclosing more of the fees pertaining to them. What they're looking at disclosing are the fees that the 401(k) plan charges. They're not going after the fees that the mutual funds in the 401(k)s are charging. But it's not as if the fund managers are trying to hide those undisclosed fees. It's just that they don't know how the year will shape up and how much trading will go on. Still, you should be aware, as an investor, that mutual funds are more expensive than they appear to be.

THE DAMAGE IN DOLLARS

We'll take $1,000 and do a quick calculation here. Let's say that for every $1,000 you've invested in a fund you think you're getting 10 percent, but you're actually only getting 7 percent. What does that three-point loss amount to in 20 years?

At 7 percent over 20 years, $1,000 will grow to $3,869. At 10 percent over the same time frame, it will grow to $6,727. So, over the course of that period, that's about a $3,000 loss for every $1,000 invested.

If you have $500,000 invested, that's close to $1.5 million that you will never see, and that's just from the fees that are sapping the value of your account. Obviously, the managers need to make their money, but fair or not, that's a big hit. People are paying those fees, along with the risk of being in the mutual fund. They might ask whether they have an alternative that didn't carry that risk and would get them the same return after fees, expenses, and taxes. I'll explain further in Chapter 9.

YOU CAN OUTGROW MUTUAL FUNDS

If you trace the growth of mutual fund assets and the growth of 401(k)s, they are like parallel train tracks. It really exploded around 1982 when the change in tax laws created the 401(k) plan and that became the plan of choice for the majority of employers. The 401(k) is the lovechild of Wall Street and the federal government. Assets started flowing into mutual funds.

Mutual funds serve a great purpose in getting people to invest. They provide economies of scale. People with less money can invest in stocks and companies to which they otherwise would not have access. By investing in mutual funds, they can buy a wide variety of stocks from different sectors and businesses. They get access and great diversification.

But you can outgrow a mutual fund. Once you reach a certain level of dollars, you need to take the training wheels off and step into the world of individual securities, monitored by a professional asset manager.

When you have over $200,000, you would be better served in the institutional-level world as opposed to the retail world of the mutual fund. It's for the same reason that you go to Costco or Sam's Club: you get better pricing. Mutual funds have layers of intermediaries who all have to be compensated: the people who sell them, the people who promote them, and the people who manage them.

At the institutional level, you take those extra hands out of the pie by going direct. You own the shares of the companies that are set up for you directly, and you pay a smaller fee to a manager who will then say, "I think we should buy this stock and sell that stock." You get rid of those other intermediaries, which means fewer fees and more money for you.

DEDUCTIBILITY OF FEES

The IRS does not recognize fees in mutual funds as a deductible investment expense. That's because the fees are buried in the rate of the return and are basically shaved off before the net asset value of a fund is calculated.

If you are able to itemize your deductions, there's a section that allows you to deduct investment expenses if, together, they equal more than 2 percent of your adjusted gross income. In the world of institutional asset management, because the fees that are charged at that level are considered investment advice, they can become a tax-deductible line item for you if held correctly.

A caveat is you can't deduct fees within an IRA, but you can if you take the fees from another account. This can be another benefit to help reduce your investment expenses if you make them tax deductible. The thing to ask yourself is whether it makes sense to make them tax deductible if you're going to pay fees anyway. Of course, you would.

I did this calculation for a client. When we moved him from the retail world to the institutional world, we saved him $9,000 in taxes by making his investment fees deductible. Like that client, you probably can think of a few fun things that you could do with $9,000. That's one example of the benefits of examining your investment fees.

Whether you have a portfolio of mutual funds or individual investments, the issue of fees combined with the issue of taxes and other charges leads to a complicated scenario that calls for expert guidance.

CHAPTER SEVEN

The Broken Stool

When you come right down to it, Social Security is a legal Ponzi scheme. The system depends upon pulling in a network of new prospects to cover those who are already in the game, and that is becoming no easy task.

It may sound harsh to describe in such a manner the venerable institution that has supported countless retirees since the era of Franklin D. Roosevelt. In most people's estimate, the government and policymakers are not akin to the investment crooks who run such schemes, and yet the principle is the same: The system takes money from some and gives it to others. It promises a return that depends on a broadening base. That pyramid tends to topple when there aren't enough newcomers at the base to support those in the levels above.

Social Security has been a mainstay of retirement planning for generations. Inaugurated in the Great Depression, it was intended as a safety net for older citizens. In the decades since, it has become part of the traditional "three-legged stool" of retirement planning.

One leg of that stool was Social Security; the others were a company pension and the retiree's own savings and investments. That was how your parents' retirement shaped up, but that stool has become wobbly, and you sit upon it at your peril.

THE STOOL OF YESTERYEAR

SOCIAL
SECURITY

EMPLOYER
SPONSORED
PLANS

RETIREMENT
SAVINGS

TODAY'S STOOL

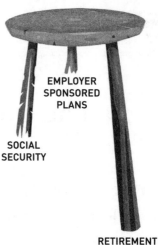

EMPLOYER
SPONSORED
PLANS

SOCIAL
SECURITY

RETIREMENT
SAVINGS

WHAT HAPPENED TO PENSIONS?

As you can see, the first leg of the "three-legged stool" is splintered and in danger of breaking. The second leg seems to have fallen off. That was the pension leg, which through the years brought retirement security to countless people.

By taking away pensions or freezing them, companies have put the responsibility for retirement success on the backs of the workers. So, not only must you be a good worker who adds value to the company, you must become a good investment manager who adds value to your retirement account. And when you reach retirement, you have to become a good pension manager.

As pensions have given way to 401(k)s and IRAs and similar plans, the third leg of the stool—your own investments—has become the only one that is intact and, perhaps, reliable. Once, personal savings were just one element of planning for retirees. Now, those savings are becoming their everything.

Your parents worked for a company for 40 or 50 years, and when they retired, they got the gold watch. The company said, "Okay, Joe, we're going to pay you $1,000 a month. If something happens to you, we're going to pay Betty $750 a month for the rest of her life. You have health care provided, and thanks for working here. Have a nice retirement," and Joe and Betty went about their merry way.

They used their personal savings for extra things such as taking a trip, visiting grandkids, buying Christmas presents. They didn't have to rely on their savings very much. Between the pension and Social Security benefit they did just fine, and their retirements were not usually as long.

Today, people entering retirement have not usually worked for a company for that long. They've switched jobs a number of times. They're not coming into retirement with any kind of company-provided pension plan.

They often have a very large amount of assets, however, the highest amount they've ever had in their lifetime, between their 401(k) and their IRA. Now they're looking at retirement as a new chapter in life. They're not planning to sit around watching *The Price is Right* until they wither and die. They have things they want to do and want the income to give them that freedom. That income now needs to come from these assets inside these retirement plans, these 401(k)s and IRAs.

That bedrock of pensions is nearly gone. What's left of it is minimal. Teachers, public officials, and some very large companies still have pensions, but by and large, they are gone, replaced by the deferred-tax plans. This evolution began in earnest around 1981–1982. All such plans, whether 401(k)s or 403(b)s and others, derive their name from their line in the tax code. Some bankers saw this as a way for the higher earners within a company to contribute more toward their retirement. So, they started looking at how to make such a provision in the tax code, and then companies started looking at it, and Wall Street started looking at it.

Wall Street began licking its chops, thinking that investors could hold money inside these 401(k)s, these great things Wall Street had created, called mutual funds. The government was setting up the parameters that allowed them to do that.

Meanwhile, corporations were looking at what was happening, and their line of reasoning was that if they set up such investment vehicles, they could get out of their responsibility to provide for their people's retirement. They could just create this plan, add some money, and offer all these investment choices. When employees left, they just took it with them. It was portable.

The employees were happy to choose their own investments—and remember that this was the 1980s when the markets were going straight up. Everyone loved his 401(k). When employees received their statements, they ripped them open and were delighted with what they saw each quarter. From 1982 to 2000 the Dow Jones expanded by over 1,000 percent, the largest bull market run we've ever seen in the history of the world. People believed they would become millionaires at retirement. "I don't need that stupid pension," they told themselves, "because I've got all this money."

As you can imagine, fewer people have had that attitude in the new millennium.

SOCIAL "SECURITY"?

When the Social Security system began, there were 43 workers to one retiree. There were plenty of young workers to support all retired workers for the few years they were likely to live after they stopped working. In 1945 each retiree had 41.9 workers supporting the benefit.

Today we have nothing close to that ratio. In 2011 that ratio was 2.9 workers for every one person taking the Social Security benefit. That's only about three people helping out each retiree, and the downward trend continues. What happens when only two workers can help you out, and then, only one?

According to a chart published by the Social Security Administration, we will reach the 2:1 ratio by 2030, and it will continue that way until 2086. The system itself acknowledges that it is in trouble. On your annual report is a disclaimer. You may have missed it. Most people just rip open the statement to see how much they will be getting. It says, in effect, that unless things change, Social Security will start paying out more than it takes in, and the trust fund will actually be exhausted by 2033. That year has been getting progressively closer. It used to be 2041, then 2038. The day of reckoning is only a generation away.

When I talk at public events, I ask people, "What percentage of the Social Security benefit do you think goes to people over age 65?" Invariably, everyone thinks it's a high percentage. It's actually around 25 percent.

The rest goes to early retirees and people on disability. The definition of a disability has become very broad. What qualifies as a disability can be quite shocking, and there are all kinds of legal entities out there that will gladly fight on your behalf to get the Social Security disability payment.

More people today are claiming their Social Security benefit early, many because they lost their job in the recession, and their unemployment ran out. Together, the payments for early retirement and for disability have increasingly stressed the system.

A STRUGGLING SYSTEM

Many people wonder whether they can count on Social Security to help them in their retirement. I have often heard them express a lack of confidence that it will be there for them at all.

In retirement planning, you can put in the figures with the assumption that things will be the same, but you want to plan for the inevitable. I think that younger people will see an increase in their full retirement age and may end up paying more in taxes. I cannot imagine, however, a big cut in benefits for retirees currently receiving them. For many, the Social Security benefit is their sole income, and it's tough enough for them already. Any effort to take away that benefit would cause a political mess. As the baby boomers enter retirement, they wield a lot of political power.

There is already a calculation on your tax form showing how much of your Social Security benefit is taxable. It's known as the Social Security tax threshold. If you are single, your benefit will become taxable if all your income sources total $25,000 or more, including half of what you get from Social Security. If you are married filing jointly, the threshold is $32,000.

In other words, you are paying a tax on a benefit that you paid a tax to get. I believe it would be easy for the politicians to write another line into the tax code mandating that if you were to reach a certain threshold, you would have to give back part of the benefit itself. The government could institute means testing to determine whether you have enough to live on and therefore don't need the benefit as much as somebody else might.

After all, there once were no thresholds. There was no taxation on any Social Security. This has all been instituted to bolster the system. We've seen the government make changes all along to prop up Social Security. The prevailing wind right now is to go after wealthy people. The government's plan of attack seems to be to claw back the benefits of people who make a lot of money, even though they paid into the system as an entitlement.

THE RISK OF RETIRING TOO SOON

People often ask what the best retirement age would be for them. There's no easy answer. If they don't like what they are currently doing, most people will tend to retire earlier. If they are happy with their jobs, they tend to retire later in life. At some point, though, people either feel they have enough money to support themselves, or they begin collecting their Social Security benefit.

In 2012, when the Employee Benefit Research Institute did a survey, it found that 24 percent of workers surveyed planned to retire before age 65. However, 65 percent of those surveyed actually did so. The trend is for people to retire earlier, either by choice or circumstance. For many, it has been the latter as a result of a downsizing. They staked their claim earlier than they had planned.

The longer you work, the longer you can live on your salary. Once you stop working, you have to use what you've accumulated, along with your Social Security benefit if you choose to claim it. Your benefit will grow by 8 percent for each year that you delay taking it. The longer you wait, the more you will get.

If you are lucky enough to have a pension, it is likely to grow too, the longer you wait, and, of course, your retirement assets will also grow, the longer you wait. That means the longer you delay retirement, the more money you could have. Since your remaining life expectancy is shorter, you are likely to have more to spend.

This is another factor in that "golden decade," the first decade of retirement when you can exert a significant influence over how your financial situation will turn out. As I pointed out earlier, these are the years before retirees are required to begin retirement plan distributions, so they have time to begin rolling them out into Roths. These are the years when you can enhance your Social Security benefit if you can delay receiving it until age 70. It won't get better after age 70. It's the same for pensions, usually: the amount you get won't increase after that age.

The longer those benefits grow, the more money you eventually will have. But what do you do for income in the meantime? That's where you could enter the realm of the tax-advantaged payout, structuring things in such a way that you could kiss the IRS goodbye for the next 10 years.

You could retire at age 60 and pay very little in income tax but still have the same amount or more of spendable income as you wait for all of these taxable accounts to come due at age 70. This is a time when you have the most control over your tax situation. It's a good time to do those strategic rollouts of 401(k)s or IRAs.

It all comes down to effective planning. If you are expecting to live a long, healthy life, you could have a lot more money coming in at age 70 if you were to delay your Social Security benefit while living on your investment proceeds and whatever you continue to earn.

I had a client who retired and had a nice mixture of assets that were both in tax-qualified plans and investments that were in taxable accounts. We were able to structure his assets in such a way that he received a high level of income so he and his wife could enjoy themselves. He was making the same income as when he was working, but he was paying 95 percent less tax. In his golden decade, until he is 70, he will continue to have a very low tax status, giving him a lot of latitude and flexibility to position assets for the future.

SOCIAL SECURITY TIPS FOR COUPLES

As people get closer to the age when they could claim their Social Security benefit, they really need to consider how to get the maximum Social Security benefit. Married couples may find this to be of particular interest. They are afforded an opportunity that single people don't have: one spouse can claim against the other spouse's record while still allowing his or her own benefit to grow.

Frequently, the strategy amounts to this: Don't claim your own benefit for now. Allow it to grow to the maximum. In the meantime, put in a claim for a spousal benefit. Your spouse's record can continue to grow if you do this right. It's a way to get free money from the IRS.

The strategy is called "file and suspend." The primary beneficiary files for the Social Security benefit but postpones receiving payments. The benefit amount continues to grow. By filing and suspending, however, these beneficiaries can now claim against their spouse's record without claiming against their own record. Meanwhile, the Social Security benefits of both spouses will continue to roll up at an 8 percent rate annually.

This works best if husband and wife are relatively close in age and both have relatively high values because both worked. Let's say the husband has a value that's worth $2,500 at full retirement age, which is 66. The wife is also 66. Her value is, let's say, $2,000. If he files and suspends, his benefit will grow at 8 percent, so at age

70 his benefit will be worth $3,401. Her benefit of $2,000 will be worth $2,720 at that time.

From 66 to 70 years of age the wife can claim half of her husband's benefit, which means half of the $2,500. They'll have $1,250 a month coming in for the next four years. That's $60,000.

You have to apply for that spousal benefit, however. It doesn't just come to you. There are many couples out there who are not availing themselves of free money. The IRS won't really tell you that. It's a nuanced thing. Some Social Security offices will, but a lot of Social Security offices won't, especially if you're in a bigger city where the office staff is inundated. They're just trying to get you through that line as fast as possible. In smaller areas, though, the Social Security people tend to have a little more time on their hands. They'll educate you on different options.

That's when you want to work with somebody who knows the strategies and has the software in place to do the calculations. A former actuary for Social Security created the software that we use. We run that calculation as part of our planning process to show clients what's available to them.

Just because the numbers point out how to get the most money from the system, that doesn't necessarily mean it's the best strategy for you. Social Security is only one leg of the three-legged stool. You need to see how it fits in relationship to other money.

You also need to consider that if you are not drawing from your Social Security benefit, you still need income. It has to come from somewhere, so it is likely to come from your assets. If you die prematurely before tapping into your Social Security benefit, that money from your assets is gone. However, if you do claim your benefit, more of your money can continue growing in your portfolio. If something happens to you prematurely, that's more that will go to the people you care about.

REPAIRING THE STOOL

So much has changed in the new millennium. People woke up to the reality that the market can also go down, and by a lot. They came to see the need to take action so they wouldn't lose a lot of what they had put together, if they hadn't lost it already. The emphasis for many has turned to making sure they don't run out of money during their lifetimes, and that is what we help people to do at my firm.

It's a given that the stool is unstable. It's a different era, and we have to be careful about how we manage our money because we don't have a big company that's going to take care of us anymore. We don't have a government that we can depend on for a benefit we can live on in retirement.

It's time to repair that broken stool so that it truly will serve you well. If you cannot put your faith in a pension, and if you have doubts about Social Security, then we need to do something with those personal savings so they can support your weight for years to come.

How do you rebuild the stool? In short, you recreate the pension leg by using some of the assets in your portfolio, while keeping enough in reserve to shore up the Social Security leg as it comes unglued from time to time. That's the beauty of the tools available today. We can replicate those pension legs for you at a very economical cost.

Used properly, those tools can create a reliable income for the rest of your life. In Chapter 9 we'll be taking a closer look at the steps you can take to forge a retirement free of financial worries.

As long as you proceed with wisdom, make good choices, and choose good counsel, you have plenty of hope.

CHAPTER EIGHT

Don't Be Worried Sick

My wife's grandmother worked as a maid at a hospital. She didn't make a lot of money but managed to raise a lot of kids. Nonetheless, she was able to accumulate a nice amount of money, which we structured to provide her a lifelong income and comfortable retirement.

She lived on her own, but eventually she began falling a lot and needed 24/7 care, which none of the children could provide. She needed to go into a skilled-care facility. I was helping to manage her assets, and we looked into acquiring long-term-care coverage, but for her, the cost was prohibitive. She had to spend down her money to pay for her care, and her children's inheritance was devoured.

Each of us faces the prospect of becoming old and frail and in need of care, and one's deteriorating health can have a debilitating effect on one's finances. It's an issue that is top of mind with many of my clients. We always address this in our discovery process.

TO INSURE OR SELF-INSURE

What it boils down to is that you make a decision on long-term care to either insure against it or to self-insure. The latter simply means you will use your own assets to pay for the care instead of the assets of an insurance firm.

In making that choice, you are deciding whether you will pay a premium to protect your assets so that they will pass on to your heirs, or else you will accept that risk and take your chances that you might never need long-term care.

People who have a large amount of assets may choose to self-insure, thinking, "I'll just pay for it out of my own pocket, and that's less money that goes to my family." One factor that goes into the decision is that you might have a spouse who still will need that money after you pass, in which case you don't want it all to go to long-term and medical care costs.

Most people of means tend to put in place some kind of insurance. The sticking point with buying long-term-care insurance is that people resist paying for something that they may not use, which might have seemed to be the case with the various insurances they have bought. In fact, they are buying something they don't want to use. To take advantage of insurance generally means something bad has happened.

Many of today's admissions to nursing homes are not for the infirmities of age. The risk that you will need long-term care is a very real one that a lot of people want to protect against. When they go to a nursing home, they do not have a condition that will kill them soon. Often, they have a degenerative disease such as dementia or Alzheimer's and could live for years.

That's probably why a lot of people procrastinate. Even if they could get long-term-care insurance in their forties or fifties, they don't want to think about that possibility. There are many more pleasant things to think about. They don't think about it until they are entering retirement, when the premiums are much larger. Then they don't do anything.

I find that people who are motivated to put protection in place are those who have seen their parents or other loved ones deplete all their assets in long-term care. People whose parents died of natural causes at home are less inclined to look into long-term care because they think, "My parents didn't need it. Why should I need it?" It's a matter of perspective.

THE MEDICAID STRATEGY

As a strategy for paying for long term-care costs, some people look to Medicaid, the state-based system for which you must be poor enough to qualify. To do so, they decide to spend down their assets.

Medicaid indeed pays for such services, but don't depend on Medicare. Some people falsely believe that their Medicare coverage will pay for long-term care. It will not. Medicare will pay for only a portion of nursing home care. It will pay only if you enter directly from the hospital, and it will pay for only 100 days. It's very limited.

Medicaid, though, pays if you are poor or once you have become poor. To qualify, some people deplete their assets on purpose in advance. In fact, one rule of thumb is that a certain level of assets should determine whether it is best to insure or deplete.

However, what is likely to happen if more and more people in our aging population choose to deplete their assets to get on Medicaid? Will the system be able to handle the onslaught? We know that Medicare has a huge liability. If you look at USDebt-Clock.org, you can see that the projected unfunded liabilities for the Medicare/Medicaid system is $80 trillion. Just like the Social

Security system, the system of Medicare and Medicaid is troubled with the prospect of becoming even more overburdened.

If you do decide that it is a good strategy to become indigent on paper by transferring assets, you must do so well in advance for it to be considered legitimate. Currently, the government can conduct a five-year "look-back" to discover when assets were transferred to your family or others.

When the government needs money, it has been known to find creative ways to get it. There have been political rumblings to institute what are known as filia laws. They are popular in Europe. In essence, the laws make people financially responsible for their families. Policy makers in some states have looked into such a law. We know that many elderly retirees lack long-term-care coverage and, eventually, will be hitting the Medicaid system. The states could institute laws to begin charging their children for some of the costs. That, of course, raises issues of fairness. In a functional family, the children might want to provide for such care, particularly if money has been transferred to them. But will children whose parents abused or abandoned them be required to pay up? Such issues are on the horizon as our system becomes ever more burdened.

LONG-TERM-CARE INSURANCE

The traditional route to protection against such costs has been to purchase a long-term-care policy. Long-term-care policies have had some issues in that their pricing was incorrect from the onset. Any type of insurance policy is based on the company's loss experience. That's how it sets the rates. Long-term care was unique in that the insurers didn't have a lot of experience when they started writing the policies.

Just a couple generations ago, families tended to provide care for their infirm parents in their homes. There wasn't a lot of care going on at institutions. In the last generation or so, society has shifted toward institutions. As insurers have paid more and more claims, they have adjusted their rates to compensate.

The increase in premiums has irritated a lot of people who took out long-term-care policies a few years ago. They thought the premium would be fixed. They didn't expect to see increases coming down the pike, and that has soured a lot of people against getting a traditional long-term-care policy.

Some have decided to forgo insurance and hope for the best. As I pointed out, some just don't see the need because they haven't experienced it in their families—yet. Others resist paying for something they might not need. If they don't go into a nursing home, those premiums never come back to them.

ALTERNATIVE COVERAGE

There's a way to get the best of both worlds—that is, protection against the high costs of care but reassurance that you won't be paying premiums to no avail. You can do so by either using asset-based models or new insurance products that I call combination policies.

The life insurance industry is very responsive to changes in demographics. It makes changes to policies to help consumers coming into the mix. Combination policies provide life insurance with accelerated benefits that can cover long-term care or chronic care.

One of two things is going to happen when you purchase this type of policy. Eventually, you will either die or require chronic or long-term care, which the policy will provide for you. Each of us has an expiration date, so something is going to happen. With a combination policy, you pay for something that's going to be used, one way or another. People feel a lot better knowing that the money they pay for coverage will go to a surviving spouse or family members as a death benefit if it isn't needed for long-term care.

You may wonder if there is a catch, but there really isn't one. The underwriting requirements are a little different from those of long-term care. They can actually be somewhat better. Remember that long-term care is written on what is called a morbidity table, which distinguishes between lethal and nonlethal illness. Life insurance is written on a mortality table.

I have had clients who were turned down for long-term care but were approved for life insurance with a long-term-care rider. Sometimes, people who can't get approved on one side can come over to the other side and get the coverage they want through one of the combination policies.

In doing so, they can protect their families and the inheritance they hope to leave. Basically, they will be able to sleep a lot better, knowing their life's work will go to something besides paying for nursing care.

There are other structured products. You can get annuity products with provisions to account for a change in your health. Some annuities will double the income stream if you end up needing long-term care or cannot perform two of the six activities of daily living. That's a nice alternative for people who want some protection but don't want to write a check every month for a standalone policy.

The insurance companies know the odds and will strive to remain profitable, but for you, as a policy holder, it can be quite a relief to know that if the worst happens, you're going to be all right financially.

Also available is a multitasker type of account, which is a combination of all three things that you want your money to do. In other words, money is available to you if you want it, money is available for long-term care or chronic care if you need it, and money will go to your heirs tax-free if you pass away. Those are wonderful policies. They reflect a more asset-based approach that incorporates a strategy for all three of those possibilities.

You can find out more about such plans and learn which would be best for your particular circumstances by talking with a knowledgeable advisor. You can simply ask, "Do you know about these types of accounts?" You will quickly see whether you are working with a retirement specialist or just an accumulation specialist.

If your advisor is not addressing these issues with you as part of your retirement plan, chances are you're working with someone who is only looking to grow your money with stocks or bonds or mutual funds. Such advisors are not worried about how you can protect against retirement risks. Your advisor should be looking holistically at your overall retirement plan.

CHAPTER NINE

Income by the Bucketful

At times, when chatting with a new client, I have found myself thinking about mayonnaise.

Long ago, back in my younger days, I took a job at an Arby's restaurant. Fast-food restaurants have what is called a speed line for making sandwiches in high volume. On that line, you have all your condiments and dressings and other makings so you can produce the fare as efficiently as possible.

One day, I was ending my shift and getting things ready for the next person when I noticed that my mayonnaise sleeve was low. It was only about a quarter full. So, I went to the cooler and got a fresh sleeve of mayonnaise. Then I began scraping into it what remained in the first sleeve.

"Why are you doing that?"

I turned to see my manager hovering over me. "I'm getting it ready to help out the next guy," I explained. "I don't want him to run out in the middle of a rush."

"Don't ever do that," he said. "He'll see that he has all this mayonnaise to spare and end up using too much. If he sees his supply is limited, he'll use less because he doesn't want to run out before the end of his shift. He'll actually use just the right amount."

When you reach retirement, you very well may have plenty of mayonnaise. Your 401(k) should have one of the biggest balances you ever had in your life. You will be tempted to look at that balance and want to slather on even more, but never forget that too much can ruin the sandwich. You could find yourself with an empty sleeve while the rush is still on. That pool of money has to last you the rest of your days. You need enough to last throughout your shift, and you don't know when quitting time will come.

A 10 PERCENT CHANCE OF FAILURE

It used to be that a 4 percent withdrawal rate was what most investment professionals prescribed for retirees. So, if you had $1 million, you could take $40,000 a year out, and your money should have a high probability of lasting 30 years in retirement.

Now, imagine you have buckled yourself into your seat on a jetliner, ready for your dream vacation, and the pilot's voice comes booming confidently over the speakers. "Good morning. We have clear skies in Los Angeles. We may encounter some turbulence along the way, but I'm currently predicting a 90 percent chance of a safe landing in Tahiti."

You might be wondering if you'll end up in the South Pacific floating in a life raft, or worse. I'm guessing you would be scrambling to unbuckle before takeoff rather than face that 10 percent chance of disaster.

That illustrates the problem that people are facing right now in using the traditional model of a 4 percent withdrawal rate on their assets. Most people would like a guarantee that they will reach their destination of a successful retirement. We want to give our clients the highest probability possible. There are tools and strategies to reach 100 percent probability that you will have sufficient income.

Your fiscal health and safety is second only to your physical health and safety. If you would be so concerned about your physical health that you wouldn't trust that pilot, then you should be as concerned about your financial health as well. Without money, you run out of options.

Just about everyone seeks a second opinion if the doctor delivers a bad prognosis. People go to whoever offers the expertise they need. They start off in life with a pediatrician, then a general practitioner, and as time passes, they see a lot of specialists. However, people don't treat their fiscal health the same way. They stay with the same general practitioner. That practitioner isn't specialized in retirement distributions and preservation. The focus is on accumulation, and as we have seen, the needs of the retiree have matured into something much different.

UPPING YOUR ODDS

The prescription for that 4 percent withdrawal rate dates to the mid-1990s. A California financial advisor, William Bengen, worked with recent retirees who were expecting to withdraw 10 percent from their portfolios annually. They felt that if they had a million dollars, what was wrong with taking out $100,000? They would still have $900,000 left, plus whatever that amount earned from the market.

Bengen conducted research in an attempt to show them that was too much money to withdraw. He developed a withdrawal rate using a Monte Carlo simulation, in which a computer program displays varying rates of return to simulate market conditions. He concluded that under a wide variety of conditions, a 4 percent withdrawal rate would allow a 90 percent probability of achieving a 30-year retirement.

On the flip side, however, that means there's a 10 percent chance it won't work. Nonetheless, sometimes, people feel discouraged and tell themselves, "I have a million dollars. I shouldn't have to live on only $40,000 a year." But remember that you also have to account for inflation and other forces that have an impact on your true rate of return.

Wall Street has followed that 4 percent standard all these years even though the fundamentals have changed. Morningstar conducted a study using today's low bond yields and low yields on cash and found that somebody withdrawing 4 percent in today's market would only have a 50 percent probability of lasting 30 years.

In other words, if you get on that plane and travel under today's conditions, there's a 50-50 chance that you could end up dead in the water. If you want to crank that up to a 90 percent probability that you will make it, you have to drop your withdrawal from 4 percent down to 2.8, which means instead of $40,000, you're only taking out $28,000. Your odds of success are still only at 90 percent, and your income is going the wrong direction.

"How could I live on that?" you may ask, especially when that three-legged stool is already so weak in its pension and Social Security legs. Some people will look at the math and say, "Well, I don't plan on living 30 years," as if that solves the problem. It's not up to them. We all need to plan for as long as possible.

You need to take longevity risk off the table. You can eliminate that risk. The types of tools available in the retirement-planning arena today can assure you a 4, 5, or even 6 percent withdrawal that is contractually guaranteed to last the lifetimes of both the husband and wife.

If there were financial tools offering a 100 percent probability of success in any economy as well as a higher withdrawal rate, when would you want to know about it? Most people would want to know right away.

THE THREE WORLDS OF MONEY

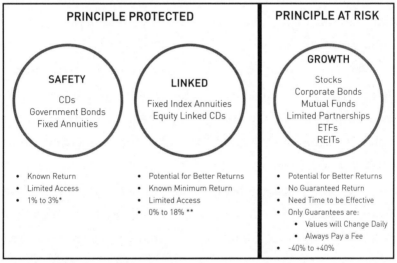

PRINCIPLE PROTECTED		PRINCIPLE AT RISK

SAFETY
CDs
Government Bonds
Fixed Annuities

LINKED
Fixed Index Annuities
Equity Linked CDs

GROWTH
Stocks
Corporate Bonds
Mutual Funds
Limited Partnerships
ETFs
REITs

- Known Return
- Limited Access
- 1% to 3%*

- Potential for Better Returns
- Known Minimum Return
- Limited Access
- 0% to 18% **

- Potential for Better Returns
- No Guaranteed Return
- Need Time to be Effective
- Only Guarantees are:
  - Values will Change Daily
  - Always Pay a Fee
- -40% to +40%

*As of the writing of this book, this is an estimate of what's available in the world of safety.

**As of the writing of this book, some strategies in the linked world could have the potential for this return.

The tools for managing your finances fall into what I call the three worlds of money. One is the world of safety, and another is the world of risk, and, since the late 1990s, we have seen a middle world developing. It's called the "linked" world.

World of Safety

The world of safety involves three entities: banks, government, and/or insurance companies.

A bank will offer you a safe instrument such as a CD or a savings account. When you buy a CD or deposit into a savings account, you know you will get the stated amount of interest for the stated amount of time. The government issues bonds and bills with the full faith and credit of the US government. The insurance companies offer fixed annuities, which function just like a CD.

The reason people want to be in the world of safety is to protect their principal. They want a known return. They want to know with certainty how much they will make. But like so many things in life, there's an advantage and a disadvantage. There is a string attached.

In the world of safety, that disadvantage often is limited access. If you take out a CD, you know that you're only going to be able to withdraw the interest that it earns. Same thing with a bond. Fixed annuities will typically allow for withdrawing up to 10 percent each year.

The disadvantage of being in that world right now is that the interest rates are pathetically low. The federal government's policy of keeping those rates low to spur economic growth has amounted to an assault on savers. Since 1982, interest rates have come down by 93 percent. It's a great time to borrow money, but when you are reaching retirement, you're not interested in borrowing anymore. You're interested in a decent rate of return.

The world of safety is not yielding much. You can get a 1 percent CD at the bank, but inflation will more than eat up that return. You might think you are being safe, but your purchasing power still is eroding.

The World of Growth

The world of growth carries risk. This is the world of investments where the institutions are the mutual fund families, the brokerage houses, and also insurance companies.

The mutual fund families, of course, will always recommend themselves. These investments have proliferated to the point where there are more mutual funds than there are investable stocks.

The brokerages promote stocks, bonds, their own mutual funds, and such instruments as real estate investment trusts and limited partnerships. They also deal in derivatives and options and all the things that Wall Street does to generate commissions.

The insurance companies offer a product called a variable annuity. It has the same last name as its brother, the fixed annuity, which is in the world of safety. But those brothers are very different. People hear the word *annuity* and think of lifelong safety, but the variable annuity places your money at risk even though you are paying for some safety provisions. It's like a duck boat. It operates on land or water—in two worlds—but it's not efficient in either. A variable annuity tries to work in the world of safety and growth, but likewise, it's inefficient in both.

The whole reason for subjecting your money to the world of risk is the potential for better returns. What you consider a better return is relative to what you once received, or to what you are used to getting. If your bank today were to offer 7 percent guaranteed on a 10-year CD, how much money would you invest in it? When I ask clients that, they all say they would put in a lot, most of their money, in fact. Could you get 7 percent on a CD at one time? Yes, as recently as 1999 or 2000, you could get 7 percent on a five-year CD. But where are those rates now?

To raise those rates will be difficult, I believe, because what happened economically in 2008 was tied to interest rates and housing. If the government raises interest rates, a whole slew of other issues will come up. Rates could remain low for the foreseeable future. Japan has had low interest rates for 20 years as it tries to spur its economy, which is what the Federal Reserve continues to do as I write this.

So where do you turn? The world of growth offers the potential for the better returns that people want but with no guarantee of principal or how much will be earned. In that world, you can be guaranteed only two things: The values will change daily, and you will always pay a fee. Whether you buy, sell, or hold, the growth world is fee laden.

To be effective in that world, you need time. Yes, you could make a nice amount. Let's say you could make 40 percent in that world in a year, but you could also lose 40 percent in a year. There's a wide range of returns, all of which are unknown.

The Linked World

About 15 years ago, the entity that works in both worlds, the insurance industry, came up with a third world, the linked world, with which most people are unfamiliar.

In the linked world, the insurance companies acknowledge that people like the world of safety, with principal protection and certainty of return, but they also like the opportunity to earn more. In the world of growth, the only thing that's really a positive is the potential. Everything else is a negative. There is no principal protection, and there is no known interest rate. Values will fluctuate, and you have the pain of fees.

The insurance companies linked the two worlds together, and basically, they borrowed a page from the Rockefellers. Back in the day, the Rockefellers would buy a US Treasury bond. They would use the interest to buy instruments in the stock market. If those investments paid off, they made money. If those investments went south, the only thing they risked was the interest. Their principal was still intact.

That's what the insurance companies did in developing these hybrid or linked products. What do they give you? Principal protection, a known minimum rate of return, but the potential for better returns, better than you can get in the other world of safety because they're linked to the performance of the stock market. If the market goes up, you make money. If the market goes down, you don't lose.

Now, the insurance companies can do something that no other entity can, and that is guarantee income for life. Banks can't do that. Mutual fund companies can't do that. Brokerage firms can't do that. The government can't do that, unless you think of Social Security that way. The only entity that can guarantee income for life is insurance companies.

At its heart, the linked world has principal protection. It has a known minimum return, but it has the potential for better returns than you could currently earn in the world of safety. It's not intended to beat the market, even though over the last 15 years a lot of policies have beaten the market. It's intended to give you a better return than what you can get in the world of safety. If the market goes up, you can participate in some of that. If the market goes down, you don't lose. On top of that, you have the additional benefit of a guaranteed lifetime income. These are the tools that can help people move from an 80 or 90 percent chance of success up to 100 percent.

ALL THREE WORLDS AT WORK

A truly diversified retirement portfolio requires a mix of investments and tools from all three worlds. You will want some of your money to stay safe and immediately accessible, while other money grows for the long term, and still other money that offers both safety and growth.

As an investor planning for retirement, you can choose your risk level and appropriately manage it. That's much of what I help my clients do. I help them come to terms with how much risk they can accept and then find vehicles to fulfill that tolerance among the different worlds of money.

Brokers will ask a client some questions and tag them as conservative, moderate, or aggressive, or somewhere in between, and treat all of their investments the same way. But all of your money must not be treated the same way. You must divvy it up among those three worlds, and how much risk you accept needs to be aligned with the intended use of that money.

LINING UP THE BUCKETS

In planning their retirement income, successful families will have a "bucket" for income, a "bucket" for growth, and a "bucket" of liquid money for emergencies and special spending. Money should be divided among those buckets to provide you with stability, safety, and predictability, while also affording a growth opportunity.

What works well in each bucket? In the income bucket, it's going to be things that are secure, such as fixed income, pension, or even this linked world. In your income bucket, you are looking for a predictable and reliable cash flow that will last for as long as you and your spouse live. In the growth bucket, you're looking for something to grow so you can outpace or keep pace with inflation and to maybe leave a legacy. In your liquid bucket, you will want cash in case the roof blows off the house or you need a new car or want to plan an extra trip. How much you should keep liquid depends on your needs and comfort level.

You'll have essential expenses and you'll have discretionary expenses in your budget. Retirees will need to replace the regular paycheck that's been coming in and have some money to play with, to use for those discretionary expenses. They need a return that hedges against inflation and balances income needs with lifestyle desires.

It all takes some finesse and a change in thinking. You need to focus on the income streams and not the lump sum of money that you are getting or that is in your portfolio. You want your principal to work for you and produce a living wage and never go away.

That's why breaking up that lump sum is so important. You must not deplete a piece of your portfolio on which you are depending for income. There's a better way, although it can be hard for people to take the steps and switch from what they have long been taught.

STEPS TO A SECURE RETIREMENT INCOME

The fundamental questions to ask yourself as you plan those retirement buckets are these: What is the difference between how much I will need each month and how much I will have? After you work out the details of that budget, you must ask yourself, what income sources will I have, how long will I need them, and what expenses do I need to pay first?

The first step, in other words, is to size up your expenses, your goals, your special needs, and your resources. What are your regular monthly bills that you simply must cover, and how much more will you need to meet the life goals that you have identified?

With all that in mind, the second step is to assess how much risk you are willing or able to accept in the market. That means two things: how much risk your portfolio can tolerate and still meet the essentials, and how much you can emotionally tolerate and still get a good night's sleep. The aim is to identify a target rate of return with as little risk as possible.

Once you have done so, you can take the step of setting up your buckets—that is, lining up your investment priorities and allocating money to them accordingly, in separate portfolio accounts.

One of those buckets should be for short-term-spending needs and living expenses, perhaps for the first five years of retirement. One of them can be for longer-term needs, as in the fifth to tenth year of retirement. This bucket can be less liquid and invested to gain a higher rate. As the first bucket empties, this one replenishes it. And another bucket can be for needs beyond the tenth year. This can be invested for even more growth, and the money will be available after a decade to replenish the earlier buckets when that time comes. You might have an additional growth bucket for risk investments and higher returns, and this one would be for optional or luxury spending or money you never intend to use.

The sooner you will need the money, the less risk you can accept. You can accept somewhat more risk for money you won't need for several years. You can take even more risk on money not needed for many years, if ever. Perhaps it's money you intend to leave to your heirs.

Why can you take that risk with longer-term accounts? It's because you are setting that money aside, confident that you won't have to touch it for years to come. If a bear market comes, your investment will be able to weather it and recover if you aren't depending on that portion of your portfolio for income. Your income needs are securely covered by your short-term buckets, with financial tools that are structurally guaranteed not to let you down in any market.

These are the steps that can bring you many a good night's sleep in retirement. You will know that you have it covered. The certainty that your money will last brings a sense of comfort that so many retirees lack as they bite their nails over the market's tribulations. Through careful planning, you can eliminate that unsettling fear that you will live too long. You deserve to enjoy a long and fruitful retirement with a legacy for the generations to come.

CHAPTER TEN

Come What May

The couple lived off the fat of their land. In their years together, they had worked hard and accumulated a lot of property, and it had increased significantly in value. The land had nourished them, providing a good income that took care of the family and their children's college educations. They were proud of what they had done, and they wanted to pass it on.

However, they had no estate plan. When I ran the numbers on the value of the land and put them up on the board, what I explained to them was that at the death of both of them, the kids would need to pay the federal government a significant amount of money in estate taxes within nine months and in cash, more money than the couple had in investments. Uncle Sam would want his cut after their death.

Where would that money come from? They didn't know. I explained that as things stood, the kids would probably be forced to sell assets just to pay the taxes due, and when you need to sell something, you often get lowballed, and normally, you don't get the best price.

That wasn't exactly this couple's dream. They envisioned their land as an asset that would serve generations to come, not as a tally on a tax bill. We had to put together a plan for them that would help ensure the land stayed in the family and the bill to the IRS was paid from the plan, not from the sale of the land.

THOSE WHO MATTER MOST

You can plan for anything. And if you don't plan, you actually still have a plan, which is that you're going to be subject to whatever tax and regulations the government has in place. Or you can plan to circumvent those pitfalls and make sure that more money transitions to the people who matter most to you.

How will your estate be managed if you become incapacitated or die? How can you pass it on to your loved ones when you want, the way you want? How can you avoid probate and minimize taxes and fees? If these are concerns that you have, this is where you need to seek professional guidance in establishing an estate plan.

Estate planning involves more than setting up the details and dealing with taxes and probate issues.

It's time to think about your desires for the generations ahead. Who and what matters most? What will be left to charity? What will be left to loved ones, to children and grandchildren?

What is the quality of those relationships, and what might that imply for passing on your wealth? Money changes people; it changes the family dynamic. You want to make sure your intentions are clearly spelled out so that there is no question as to what you want to have happen.

Such is the swirl of considerations that you need to distill into a proper and sensible estate plan.

NOT JUST AN ISSUE FOR THE RICH

Many people, when considering these issues, turn their thoughts first to the possibility that they will be hit by an estate tax. The estate tax doesn't affect as many people as you might think. The estate tax exemption level currently is about $10.5 million for a married couple. It wasn't too long ago that the estate tax kicked in on assets over $675,000.

The estate tax used to be called the death tax. People don't like the idea of being taxed at death, but the estate tax doesn't affect a lot of people. What can affect everyone is the removal of the step-up in basis. Right now, capital assets enjoy a step-up in basis. If you own some stock or a piece of land, and you pass away and leave it to your heirs, its value will step up to its value at the date of your death.

If that is removed, the value for them, when they go to sell that asset, will go back to what you originally paid for it. Very easily, our government could eliminate the step-up in basis and generate a tremendous amount of tax revenue. Your heirs would owe a long-term capital gains tax on all that gain. As it stands, with the step-up in basis, if they sold the asset on the day after your death, there would be no gain, so they would have no tax issue. I expect that this will be one of the changes that the government will make to get more tax revenue.

These are all political issues. These policies can be changed with a piece of legislation, which could be a popular move since people think this is something that affects only the very rich. Yes, the rich are politically powerful, but this affects more than the very rich. It can affect people who didn't consider themselves rich but who may have more in gains and in assets than they thought they did when it comes to figuring out what belongs to the estate.

The general population is in favor of going after the rich. The problem is that your definition of rich and the government's definition are entirely different. In this era of the millionaire next door, we need to look closely at what goes into an estate. It's more than the value of the house and car.

For example, the proceeds from life insurance, though not taxable as income, could be considered part of the estate value if held incorrectly and could push you closer to the exemption threshold, or above. That's why you must plan to have it be held outside your estate, and there are different ways in which you can do that. One of the primary strategies that helps offset estate tax or helps to avoid paying it unnecessarily is life insurance. It is a powerful tool that can overcome a lot of estate tax issues.

A JOB FOR AN ATTORNEY

As we discuss trusts and the various other important elements of estate planning, let me make it clear that the documents establishing these entities must be drawn up by practicing attorneys. I'm not an attorney. I do understand the laws, but you will need an attorney who has the authority to draw up those trusts, wills, powers of attorney, and more.

We work with a network of professionals, including such attorneys, who treat our clients well and can get the appropriate documents in place for them. If you have your own lawyer, we will work with that person.

In our estate plan review, we make sure that what you need is set up appropriately. A lot of people have a trust, and we try to make sure it is funded. Otherwise, it's like buying exercise equipment that you take out of the box but never use. A trust is no good unless you use it, and the way to use it is to fund it.

Just going to an attorney and paying a couple thousand dollars to get a nice leather-bound binder that documents your trust doesn't mean anything until you've actually executed it. That's one reason to beware of the do-it-yourself type of trusts and wills that you might find online. You can accomplish some things that way, but you really need professional guidance or you can end up with a trust that's meaningless. Again, if it's not funded, what's the point?

DOCUMENTS YOU MAY NEED

Let's take a look at some of the important documents that people need to start thinking about and getting in order for their estate planning.

An essential one is a power of attorney. It grants somebody else the authority to do something on your behalf. You really need two types. You need a power of attorney for financial matters and a power of attorney for health care. Once you become incapacitated, you can't grant powers of attorney. That's why it's imperative that you get those in place beforehand.

At the very minimum, you need a will. But a will is going to take you through probate to assign the ownership. Probate is going to be the public court system, which will expose your estate to prying eyes and creditors and all kinds of delays and expense. Probate is a drawn-out legal exercise that's going to delay your estate and publicize the proceedings, so people whom you don't know or don't care about are going to know what you had and who got it. It's best to avoid it, if possible, and to minimize the tax and fees that result. Some things don't need to go through probate, such as life insurance, and qualified plans such as IRAs, or 401(k)s. For anything for which you can name a beneficiary directly, you should not have to go through the probate process as long as that beneficiary is named correctly.

With a trust, in essence, you are doing what the probate court does, but you're doing that in advance. After you assign ownership to an asset, it doesn't have to go through probate. You can transfer money to people or entities that you care about and keep it private. There are revocable living trusts and irrevocable living trusts. "Revocable" means you can make changes; "irrevocable" means you can't. The one you choose will depend on your particular situation.

Sometimes, people confuse the terms *living trust* and *living will*. The latter is a health-care directive stating that you do not want to be kept alive by artificial means. That, too, is an essential document, because once you are incapacitated, it's too late.

You can readily find detailed definitions and distinctions for each of these estate-planning tools. Your circumstances will determine what is best for you, and a qualified advisor can help you decide. Like all tools, trusts are powerful if used correctly, and they are right for some tasks and for some people but not for others.

IS A WILL THE WAY?

If you have set up a will, you may be wondering about the relative advantage of a trust and whether it would make sense for your financial situation.

A will becomes activated at your death, so basically, it's the tool to direct your assets to the people and places that you care about after your death. A trust, however, is a tool that you can also use while you're alive. Trusts are multifaceted and can be used in a variety of ways, while you are here and after you are gone.

Besides being used to avoid probate problems and to reduce the impact of estate taxes, trusts can also be set up to protect assets from creditors. Trusts can be used for Medicaid planning, as well, and they can direct assets to certain heirs with restrictions on when they will receive the money and how they can use it. Even after you die, you can have a say in making sure those who inherit your money will be good stewards of it.

THE EXPENSE OF A TRUST

A trust is going to cost more up front because the attorney has to draft it. The cost could range from a couple thousand dollars for uncomplicated ones to perhaps as much as $10,000. It all depends on your situation and the complexity.

It's worth every penny when you can consider how much the document can save you and your heirs in the long run. The probate expenses for a will can be high. Here in Iowa, most of the time, a flat 2 percent will go to the attorneys. That's 2 percent of the entire estate. So, if between your home and your money you have half a million dollars at 2 percent, that's $10,000 in fees. Where a trust may have cost you $2,000 to set up, your heirs will be grateful, because they are the ones who would have paid those probate costs.

CHARITABLE GIVING

As you contemplate the meaning of your life's work, you will likely be considering who and what has been most meaningful to you, not only family members but institutions and causes as well. Charitable giving is a key element of estate planning for many.

The principle to always keep in mind, if you have charitable intentions, is this: Charities are tax-exempt organizations. When you look at your assets, you will probably see that some of it is taxed heavily, or tax-toxic, as we call it. That will include all of your qualified plans, your 401(k)s and IRAs. You will also have assets that do not carry those tax consequences. That could be things such as your real estate, money in the bank, and life insurance. When donating money to others, whether before or after your death, give the tax-toxic assets to those who do not pay tax.

Remember that for all of your IRAs and 401(k)s and other tax-deferred plans, there are two beneficiaries: your family (or whomever you have named) and the government. The government will want its cut. But the government also has agreed that charities do not pay tax. Therefore, if you leave your money to a charity, you erase the government's claim on the money.

Let's use the example of a 70-year-old couple who have $500,000 in an IRA but do not need the money to live on. They want to leave the money to their children, so they take out only RMDs. In the first year, their minimum distribution on $500,000 is $18,250.

What can they do with that money? One of three things: they can spend it, save it, or leverage it. If they save it, they have one of two ways to save it. They can save it in a taxable fashion, or in a tax-deferred fashion.

If they save it in the taxable fashion, it's going to add more tax to them every year going forward. If they save it in a tax-deferred fashion, they're going to create more tax down the road when the asset comes out at their death.

Or they can leverage it by shifting the money into a tax-free account, such as life insurance. By leveraging it, the couple can create a pool of tax-free money that can help to equalize the inheritance to the family. That way, the tax-toxic IRA can go to the charity, which will not pay tax on it, and the only entity that loses is the government.

Such strategies are quite possible and commonly accomplished, but setting up such arrangements as part of your retirement and estate planning calls for careful consideration of their overall effect on your finances. You will want professional guidance as you undertake these measures, but if you do this properly, you can effectively disinherit Uncle Sam and leave more for your loved ones.

THE Ds OF ESTATE PLANNING

Life changes, often slowly and sometimes swiftly. Trusts and all kinds of estate planning documents need to be reviewed regularly, and that is particularly important if you move from state to state. Your trust may need to be updated in your current state.

As a quick reference to when these documents should be reviewed, we refer to the Ds of estate planning, which, for the most part, are self-explanatory. The Ds stand for decade, death, divorce, dependent, disability, and discharge.

You should review all the changes in your life at least once each decade. Circumstances, priorities, and goals change, and you will want your estate plan to be appropriately updated.

You should review your documents upon the death of anyone who plays a significant role in your estate plans. For example, what would happen if one of your children were to die? Would you be willing to let the money go to an immature grandson?

If you were to divorce, or if any of your children were to divorce, you likewise would want to take a close look at your documents. It is likely that you would want to change the beneficiaries of insurance coverage, retirement funds, annuities, and the like. Who is named in your will or trust? Who has power of attorney?

Has there been a change in any of your dependents? Do you wish to help them or other descendents with any needs they are facing? Perhaps a grandchild needs money for college. What's the best way to contribute?

Have you or anyone else in your estate plan experienced a disability or a diagnosis of health problems? You could face a situation in which you might want to set up a special needs trust for a loved one.

Have you been discharged from work? By that, I mean separated for whatever reason, whether a layoff or retirement. This is another life-changing event that is going to affect your estate plan.

MAKE YOUR INTENTIONS CLEAR

To help ensure that your wishes will be carried out upon your passing, you should keep those who matter most to you apprised of your intentions. Family meetings are an excellent way to keep those lines of communication open.

In our practice, when we set up a new client's retirement plan, we give them a binder with all their important information organized. One of the first things the client will see upon opening that binder is a letter with a big stop sign on it.

That letter is for the beneficiaries to find. It warns that if these accounts are not treated correctly, they could be subject to a lot of unnecessary taxation. The letter urges the beneficiaries to contact the advisor regarding their options. In effect, you will be speaking to them from beyond.

You will want to tell them these things from the here and now as well. You worked hard for your money. You want your heirs to know that you expect them to explore their options and treat that money with respect, in honor of all you sacrificed to help change their lives for the better.

Peace, Freedom, Impact

In the caves of the cliffs of Kona, out on the Big Island of Hawaii, the natives once placed the remains of the tribal chieftains. There, high above the water, nobody could desecrate their secret resting place.

To accomplish this, the high priest would select a child from the village. That child would be lowered over the edge by a rope to place the bones in the cave. Then, the chief would cut the rope, and the child would plummet to his death on the jagged rocks.

In that culture it was an honor bestowed upon the family for a child to be so chosen. This was a matter of family heritage and pride. The sacrifice was respected, and the family rose in esteem in future generations.

Today we eschew such practices, but our desire to elevate our families and build a respected legacy is as strong as ever. Money matters immensely, but it is not everything. Retirement planning has much to do with how best to handle the money, but it also involves building that legacy.

These matters are heavy on the minds of many people, particularly as they get older. They think about passing on their values and their ethics. They want to leave behind the story of who they were and what they believed.

We all have a personal story, whether we know it or not, and when we share those stories, others gravitate to us. Many of us have never taken the opportunity to share with our children the story of how our lives were when we ourselves were children. We haven't traced for them the trials and triumphs along the way. But it is in such sharing that you can engender a deep appreciation for what you have created.

Think about it. You did some fine things in your life. We've all walked a different path, but each of us has something special and unique to offer and lessons to impart. To pass on your story is a gift beyond measure. It is important for each of us to safeguard not only our money but also our reputation so that we have much of value to contribute to posterity.

Though we do not resort to burial caves on the precipice to keep away the tomb raiders, we do wish to keep away anyone or anything that would detract from our goals. We do not sacrifice humans, but we devote the time and energy to plan carefully for the future. We must not let our graves be plundered.

Each of us carries for a lifetime the values instilled early on. How we feel about money is planted early. I remember vividly those scenes from the salon, where I lay waiting for my mother to finish her shift. I recall the animated conversations, the plans, the dreams. Some of those ladies struggled, I'm sure, but mostly I could sense their joy as they talked about their families and the places they would go and all they would do.

They had peace of mind. They felt a sense of freedom and financial security that would last them the rest of their lives. And that is what I wish for our clients today: the freedom to pursue what matters most in life, knowing that they will be all right to the very end.